KAUAI RESTAURANT GUIDE 2005

WITH POIPU BEACH

Robert & Cindy Carpenter
www.hawaiirestaurantguide.com

KAUAI RESTAURANT GUIDE 2005
WITH POIPU BEACH

1st Edition

Copyright © 2005, by Robert & Cindy Carpenter

All rights reserved. No part of this publication may be reproduced or transmitted in any form or by any electronic or mechanical means, including the use of information storage and retrieval systems, except brief extracts for the purpose of review, without the written permission of the publisher and copyright owners.

ISBN 1-931752-34-6
Library of Congress Control Number: 2005924690

Every effort has been made in the preparation of this work to assure that the information contained herein is as accurate and timely as possible. However, as changes can occur neither the authors nor the publisher assumes or accepts any responsibility or liability for any losses, charges, damages, or disruptions of any kind for any reason associated with the use of the material included in this book.

Printed in the United States of America.

Holiday Publishing Inc.

Post Office Box 211
Havana, IL 62644

Post Office Box 11120
Lahaina, HI 96761

holidaypublishing@yahoo.com

www.hawaiirestaurantguide.com

KAUAI RESTAURANT GUIDE 2005
WITH POIPU BEACH

TABLE OF CONTENTS

Hawaiian Islands

Kauai

Oahu

Molokai

Lanai

Maui

Kahoolawe

Hawaii

INTRODUCTION

It's been said that there are those who eat to live and those that live to eat. Since you're reading this you probably already have a leaning toward the latter group. Well, join the club! Food has taken on an importance never seen before. That's not to say that Mom's cooking wasn't good. What better place can you think of to develop your own sense for comfort food than at the kitchen table? However, with restaurants popping up on every corner and 24 hours of food shows airing daily, culinary pursuits have definitely come of age.

Hawaii is a perfect place to explore this newfound enthusiasm. Here in the islands you'll find people from around the world blending and sharing the best of their cultures. Naturally the local dining scene reflects this international view where noodle shops and Continental dining venues make perfectly compatible neighbors. Then to make things that much more interesting, Hawaii people like to throw in some fusion cuisine and a little contemporary sushi to complete the neighborhood mix. You won't find that back in Ohio!

This book was written in an attempt to define this wonderful disarray. Knowing full well that this was a nigh on impossible task we took off happily into the fog and aren't quite sure if we've emerged yet! Let's just say that five years, six islands, and 1500 assorted restaurants, dining spots, and take-out windows later, you now have in your hands a copy of the 2005 Kauai edition of the Hawaii Restaurant Guide series.

Along the path of creation we've found ourselves doing a bit of experimenting. Before putting pen to paper there first had to be research, which of course was our favorite part of the undertaking. Being self-confessed culinary vagabonds, what better way to combine our vices than an extended dining tour across the Hawaiian Islands? As the adventure continued, it started taking on a bit of a Keseyian spin. When the term fusion confusion became part of our vocabulary, we knew it was time to state a criterion. Here is what we determined.

Experience has shown us that our readers want to be empowered. They don't care for travel experiences that include being shoved on a bus and handed a meal voucher. Nor do they like being led around to all the standard guidebook hot spots. No, they want to go it alone and make their own decisions, so we resolved to arm them with as much information as possible.

To start with, people need to have accurate information concerning the physical location, website address, phone number, hours of operation, dress code, style of cuisine, credit cards, and price range of each establishment. Then they like to see actual menu items with prices to determine budgeting. What might be medium priced to one person could be something entirely different to another.

Our restaurant selection process follows suit. We decided early on not to waste time writing about places we wouldn't bother revisiting and skipped right to creating an A list. Why waste time beating up on also-rans when there are so many wonderful places to talk about? The results have been assembled in a collection that covers all tastes and styles from five stars to hole-in-the-walls.

Of course no restaurant guide would be complete without impressions. People have repeatedly told us that they want to know what to expect before they arrive. This can run the gamut from dealing with parking to personal preferences like waterfront dining. In our comment sections we try to deal with real world issues and leave the chamber of commerce spin to the paid inclusion publishers.

Finally, all of this was done at our own expense. Too much of what readers encounter is slanted by compensation. In the world of travel, that comes in many forms. It could be through free rooms, complimentary meals, or outright cash payment. Regardless, the resulting work becomes an advertorial instead of an unbiased review. It's hard to be objective when they roll out the red carpet!

So plan to visit Hawaii! Explore the renowned pleasures of sights and sounds to be found in the islands. But while you're there, be sure to discover some of the culturally diverse culinary experiences unique to America's Pacific Paradise!

Robert & Cindy Carpenter
Authors

ISLAND
CUISINES

HAWAIIAN CUISINE

It has been said that everybody in Hawaii came from someplace else which also holds true for many of the food sources we think of as native to the island chain. The Hawaiian Islands are geologically very young. They are also among the most remote places on earth with nearly three thousand miles of open ocean separating the islands from any major land mass. Hawaii's youth and isolation led to the evolution of a unique but nutritionally sparse flora and fauna.

The first arrivals in Hawaii are thought to have been a small dark people whose origins hail back to Southeast Asia. Archaeologists believe that these people lived off what they found which didn't go much beyond fish, birds, and a few native plants. Many like to think of those earliest inhabitants as the legendary Menehune, but they, like their history, disappeared into the annals of time. It wasn't until the Polynesians voyaged to Hawaii with their domestic animals and "canoe" plants that the island food resources achieved any variety.

These ancestors of the modern Hawaiians were great mariners. A thousand years ago they began sailing their double-hulled voyaging canoes up from Tahiti bringing with them dogs, pigs, and fowl as well as coconuts, sweet potatoes, breadfruit, bananas, taro, yams, arrowroot, and sugarcane. They also brought the Polynesian style of cooking which includes broiling over hot coals, boiling with hot stones, and baking in an underground oven. It is this latter method, cooking in an imu, that holds center stage at Hawaiian luaus today.

Ancient Hawaiians lived in ahupua'a which were land divisions reaching from the top of the mountains down adjoining ridges to the ocean. These triangular watersheds theoretically contained all the elements required to sustain the community. Trees for building canoes grew up on the mountain. The uplands supported dry land crops like sweet potatoes and yams. Down along the stream beds taro was grown in paddies called loi. Then, beyond the coconut and breadfruit trees, lay the ocean with its wealth of fish, mollusks, and seaweeds.

The Hawaiian diet was simple but healthful. Fish provided the bulk of the common people's protein with domestic animals and fowl reserved primarily for the chiefs and special occasions. The staple starch was poi made from the steamed and pounded corms of the taro plant. When conditions wouldn't allow for taro cultivation sweet potatoes or breadfruit were used as substitutes. Taro greens and seaweed filled the need for leafy vegetables by supplying vitamins and minerals. Finally, bananas and coconuts were important for good health.

Today these traditions continue. Modern Hawaiians usually cook much like everyone else, but they make a point to hold luaus to celebrate milestones in life. Island favorites like kalua pig, lomi lomi salmon, chicken long rice, laulau, haupia, and of course poi are staples at these events. If you get the chance, try to attend a luau and experience the original Hawaiian cuisine.

CHINESE CUISINE

The Chinese have influenced the socio-economic and culinary scenes of the islands to the point that it would be hard to imagine Hawaii without them. Beginning in the mid 1800's they were the first immigrant group recruited to work in the sugar cane fields. From those humble beginnings the Chinese went on to become the merchant class and landlords of Honolulu.

The Chinese experience in Hawaii is more than a list of menu items and real estate investments. It's a meaningful part of Hawaiian history. The early Chinese immigrants came from southern China, so naturally they brought that style of cooking with them. After they arrived it didn't take long for them to figure out that there wasn't much of a future working on the plantations, so as soon as their contracts expired they moved on.

These free but unemployed farmers looked around and saw opportunity. Where the Hawaiians had once raised taro and fish the Chinese saw rice paddies and duck ponds. Intermarriage provided access to idle land that soon became truck gardens and small farms. Since trading is a way of life for the Chinese, the port of Honolulu quickly had its own Chinatown full of shops and small eateries.

Today you see the effects of this history throughout the islands. The dominant Chinese cuisine in Hawaii is Cantonese. This is what most North Americans picture when they think about eating Chinese, so the methods and menu items are quite well known. Preparations like dim sum and stir-fries are popular in that region and are standards on menus in Hawaii.

True Chinese cooking is a healthful cuisine. Chefs in China instinctively strive for balance and harmony in meal preparation. This can be accomplished by using a variety of cooking methods and ingredients. No Chinese cook would ever serve an entire deep-fried meal; rather he or she would always include vegetable dishes and serve steamed rice on the side.

To fully enjoy a Chinese meal make sure you choose a variety of dishes, levels of spiciness, and cooking methods. This is dining banquet style, but it can still be done at a fairly reasonable cost. Some restaurants have made things easier by selecting an assortment of dishes and offering them as a package, but those set menus can be a bit on the middle-of-the-road side. Make your meal an adventure and select the items yourself—just watch out for the chicken feet!

No trip to Honolulu is complete without a visit to Chinatown. Take a walk and look for the shops with the barbequed pork and smoked ducks hanging in the windows. Down off King Street you'll find markets packed with people selling vegetables you've never seen and fish so fresh they're still swimming. Finally, stop for lunch at a place where you're the only ones speaking English and there isn't a fork in sight. That's when you'll know why they call it Chinatown.

JAPANESE CUISINE

Like so many others the Japanese experience in Hawaii is tied to sugar. The first immigrants began arriving from Japan soon after the end of the American Civil War. At first it was a trickle, but after the Reciprocity Act Of 1876 removed tariffs on Hawaiian sugar, the trickle turned into a torrent. That was the age of industrialized sugar, and enormous amounts of manpower were required. Today Americans of Japanese ancestry play a major role in Hawaiian society. This is reflected through Hawaii's wide variety of Japanese dining venues.

It has been said that the Japanese eat with the eyes as well as the mouth. This becomes apparent after visiting one of their restaurants. Instead of having a single main entrée dominating the table, Japanese diners prefer a variety of smaller servings. The dishes are served separately on various plates and bowls artistically arranged around the table.

The ultimate fine dining experience is the kaiseki. This is also known as royal dining or dining in courses and involves considerable ceremony as well as an elegant dinner presentation. An elaborate array of special courses is served that might include items such as an exquisite appetizer, assorted sashimi and sushi, miso soup, a tempura course, a seafood dish, a small steak, pickled vegetables, steamed rice, cold noodles, and dessert.

A more common choice is the teishoku or complete meal. This Japanese equivalent of the prix fixe dinner consists of an appetizer, soup, pickled vegetables, one or two entrees, rice, and perhaps dessert. Anyone interested in exploring Japanese cuisine would do well to start with a teishoku as the variety allows the diner to do some sampling and not be overwhelmed by the menu.

Within the various meal presentations you will find a variety of preparation styles. Thanks to the spread of international dining, visitors to Hawaii often think of sushi and sashimi as typical Japanese food. While those are popular items in Japan, their cuisine goes far deeper than that. Beyond the temptations of the sushi bar you will find several major styles of cooking.

First comes yakimono, which are grilled or broiled dishes. Teriyaki and yakitori are classic examples of yakimono. That knife-wielding chef in a teppanyaki house is also doing a form of yakimono cooking. Then there's agemono where meats or vegetables are fried in oil. Tempura with its light puffy coating is probably the most recognizable form of agemono. Finally you have nabemono where thinly sliced pieces of meat and vegetables are gently simmered in a fragrant broth using a chaffing dish placed on the tabletop. Shabu shabu and sukiyaki are traditional nabemono dishes.

So walk into a Japanese restaurant with confidence, and after a half-bow to the hostess get ready for a truly unique and exceptional dining experience.

15

PORTUGUESE CUISINE

Portuguese culinary tradition is the odd man out among ethnic cuisines in Hawaii. Where all the rest are Asian in origin Portuguese is European. When the Asians serve a starch it is nearly always rice. For the Portuguese starch means bread or beans. Asians love stir-fries. The Portuguese prefer stews. In spite of all these differences, Portuguese cooking has become a valued part of the Hawaiian melting pot.

The Portuguese have always been a seafaring people. During the fourteenth and fifteenth centuries Portuguese ships embarked on a great wave of global exploration. Those adventurers brought back spices and foods that were unheard of in Europe. The resulting trade routes reached around the world exposing the Portuguese to exotic places and exotic places to the Portuguese.

The first Portuguese plantation laborers arrived in Hawaii during the 1870's and were actually from the Azores and Madeira. This was a rather natural development as sugarcane had been part of the Madeira agricultural scene for hundreds of years. These European immigrants differed from their Asian counterparts as they intended to stay in Hawaii permanently. Their families brought hearth and home along with the entire range of Portuguese cuisine.

Hearty soups, stews, and casseroles were a rather new concept in the islands but old favorites among the Portuguese. Usually these were enhanced with the wide variety of spices and flavors that had come into their possession through global exploration. Portuguese sausage or linguica with its garlicky zest has gone on to become a mainstay breakfast item across the islands. In Hawaii you'll find eggs and Portuguese sausage right next to Egg McMuffins and breakfast burritos on fast food restaurant menus.

Another island favorite is Portuguese Bean Soup. If Hawaii people had to name the recipes that make their top ten list, Portuguese Bean Soup would be there every time. Somehow it doesn't seem to matter what a restaurant normally serves or where its price range falls, this local comfort food combining beans and vegetables with ham hocks and Portuguese sausage manages to make its way into the rotation as soup of the day.

Finally, there is the Portuguese tradition of baking bread. Everywhere you go in Hawaii you'll find menus offering French toast made with Portuguese sweet bread. Also known as pao doce, this local favorite has taken on another identity as Molokai Sweet Bread. Visitors to that island will see local people boarding the plane carrying loaves for those at home. Another Portuguese specialty is the sugary doughnut without a hole known as the malasada. Traditionally served as a special treat the day before Ash Wednesday, malasadas were prepared using the family's remaining butter and eggs before starting the lean times of Lent.

KOREAN CUISINE

Immigrants from Korea began arriving in Hawaii during the early 1900's. Like their fellows, the early arrivals came to work on the plantations. Although that era is all but over, the migration continues today as Koreans seeking economic opportunity leave their homeland for Hawaii and other parts of North America.

Koreans strive for balance and harmony in all aspects of their lives. This is never more obvious than at the table, where they look to food as a cure for physical and mental ailments as well as for sustenance. Their cuisine is low in fat and very healthful with an emphasis on grilled or broiled meats, soups, and fresh vegetables. Some of the cooking methods favored by Koreans involve tableside preparation using a grill or by simmering meats and vegetables in broth, while others require pan or deep-frying.

One item that has almost come to mean Korean is kim chee. Interestingly enough both of this pickled relish's principal ingredients came from other places. The Dutch introduced cabbage to the Koreans and the chili peppers that give kim chee its fire were brought from Portugal. This zesty condiment is nearly always seen on Korean tables and adds zip to offset the mildness of rice.

Contrary to general impressions not all Korean food is highly seasoned. In fact many of their favorite menu items could pass as comfort food. If you like teriyaki then you'll enjoy the marinated grilled meats. Koreans are more of a beef-eating nation than other Asian countries. It is thought that invading Mongols introduced cattle to Korea hundreds of years ago. Other protein sources common to the Korean diet include poultry and fish as well as soybean products.

For those who really like to know the details, some of the ingredients used as flavoring in Korean cuisine include chrysanthemum leaves, daikon, ginger root, garlic, enokitake, shimeji and shiitake mushrooms, hot green and red peppers, green onions, mirin, miso, nori, sesame oil and seeds, pine nuts, soybean sprouts, soy sauce, tofu, and wakame.

Combination meals are usually offered giving the diner a chance to experience a variety of items. These dinners begin with several small dishes of salads and pickled vegetables. Turnips, potatoes, kim chee, seaweed, bean sprouts, and garlic bulb pickles among others will be offered. Soup made of oxtails, fish, chicken or vegetables, many times with the addition of a beaten egg or dumplings, are important courses in a Korean meal. Popular entrées commonly seen include bulgoki, kal bi ribs, and chun. As in other Asian cultures desserts are limited to fruits and special occasion items.

Most island Korean restaurants tend to be less formal establishments where one can enjoy a healthful dinner of wonderfully prepared foods at a reasonable cost.

17

FILIPINO CUISINE

Filipinos constituted the last major group of immigrants recruited to work on Hawaii's sugar cane and pineapple plantations. Their arrival during the early to mid-1900's was a reaction to legal restrictions placed by the US Congress on importing foreign workers. The Hawaiian planters needed cheap field labor, and as the Philippines were a US Territory, it became the logical alternative.

Although at first glance one might assume that Philippine culture would be Southeast Asian in nature that is not at all the case. Early visits from the east followed by three hundred years of Spanish occupation and fifty years as a US Territory heavily influenced Filipino daily life. The result is a cuisine that is truly global in nature.

Early traders from China and Malaysia are thought to have been the first outsiders to seriously impact the culinary traditions of the Filipino people. The use of egg roll wrappers in lumpia, rice, curry, coconut, coconut milk, patis, soy sauce, and noodles all had their origins in eastern cuisines.

Then came the Spanish who truly made an impression on the daily diet in the Philippines. Tomatoes, onion, garlic, beans, pimientos, and olive oil have become everyday components in Filipino dishes. During the late 1890's America was at war with Spain and the islands came under US military rule. Although Filipino people enjoy American dishes as well as their own, little of what we consider true Filipino food could be attributed to that period of history.

Today the Filipino influence on the culinary arts in Hawaii might not be as noticeable as that of some other Asian cuisines as there are not many restaurants serving an exclusively Filipino menu. However, that doesn't mean that visitors won't be exposed to Filipino food. Many island restaurants incorporate Filipino styles and dishes in their menus. You just have to know what to look for.

Filipino cooks like to mix all of a dish's ingredients together rather than preparing and serving them separately. A classic example of this is adobo, which is a stew made from pork and/or chicken that has been marinated in garlic and vinegar. Another is chicken relleno, which is a roasted and boned chicken that is stuffed with a pork, onion, raisin, pimiento, and hard-cooked egg stuffing.

Then come the veggies! Filipino culinary tradition calls for the use of an extremely wide variety of vegetables. Most Western visitors won't easily identify many of them, but a walk through a Filipino grocery or Chinatown will give you the idea. Of course, no meal would be complete without rice or pancit noodles to round things out.

Finally, the Filipinos are fond of sweets. Look for leche flan, fruit lumpia, or cascaron and you'll know you've found the dessert section of the menu.

THAI CUISINE

People from Thailand were among the first modern immigrants who did not come to Hawaii seeking work on the plantations. Their arrival over the last thirty years was part of a general movement out of Southeast Asia by those looking for more promising forms of economic opportunity. As many before them had already discovered, a quick way to create an income in a new land is to open a restaurant and introduce the neighborhood to your native cuisine. Hawaii with its large Asian ethnic population was a natural for these new entrepreneurs. Thai cuisine has quickly become a local favorite.

Thai cuisine reflects an interesting history of interaction between people throughout Indochina. Thanks to its central location Thailand became a crossroad for foreign travelers and exotic ideas. Immediately to the north lies China with its ancient traditions of stir-frying and the use of noodles. Among that group were Buddhists preparing vegetarian dishes. From the west came people from India making curries and Arabs cooking skewer-broiled meats. And of course don't forget the ever-present Portuguese and their tiny red hot peppers!

Chefs from Thailand have a whole arsenal of flavors at their disposal. Some of the ingredients commonly used include Thai chilies, Kaffir lime leaves, lemon grass, ginger, mint, basil, curry, peppers, and the ever-present fish sauce known as nam pla. Thai food may be ordered spiced mild, medium, or hot. However, since mild dishes can miss the point and hot is best reserved for the Thai's we suggest that people consider ordering medium. Then in order to moderate the spicy flavors, be sure to include at least one dish that is made with coconut milk and have it all served along side a steamer basket of sticky rice.

A meal in a Thai restaurant is generally served all at once and then shared between the diners, rather than in courses. Usually a number of dishes are presented giving everyone an opportunity to sample a variety of items. Great effort is made to balance out the contrasting tastes and textures in order to promote harmony in the meal. Unlike many Asian countries a fork and spoon are used in dining. The fork is used for cutting and pushing food onto the spoon, and the spoon gives the diner the ability to fully appreciate the flavorful sauces.

A good rule to follow in making dinner selections is to always ask, "What do the locals order?" Here there are favorites like anywhere else. Starting with the appetizer section consider the Thai Crispy Noodles or Satay Chicken. Then follow up with a Green Papaya Salad and a bowl of Tom Yum Soup. Next comes the main event where dishes like Evil Prince Shrimp, Pork Pad Pet, Chicken Panang Curry, and Beef with Thai Basil Sauce appear high on the list. Finally, make sure to include a dish of Pad Thai Noodles and dinner is served.

Try to visit a Thai restaurant while in you're in Hawaii. You'll discover an exciting new cuisine that truly broadens the horizons of culinary adventure.

VIETNAMESE CUISINE

The end of the Vietnam War signaled the beginning of a major migration of Vietnamese people to Hawaii and North America. What started out as a political exodus has turned into a classic movement of people seeking a better way of life. Hawaii has been an attractive location for resettlement because of its mild, temperate climate and the presence of other Asian cultures. Today their presence has become so visible that there are those who refer to the central part of the Honolulu Chinatown historic district as Little Saigon.

While you are walking around Chinatown notice the small Vietnamese eateries that seem to be popping up on every street corner. At one time, Chinese immigrants operated these shops. Now those people have moved on to other endeavors and the latest wave of arrivals have taken their place. Many of these places are pho shops. Pho is pronounced "fuh" and is an aromatic rice noodle soup made with a clear, rich beef stock. A plate of fresh herbs such as Thai basil and cilantro along with bean sprouts and jalapeños is served on a separate plate. You flavor this popular breakfast or lunch dish to your own specifications.

Vietnamese cuisine is the result of many years of cultural blending. Like the other countries in Southeast Asia, the ebb and flow of history brought in successive waves of new people and customs. The original inhabitants of Vietnam are thought to have moved down the coastline from southern China. Then others from the east and west arrived looking for trade. There were occupations, first by the Chinese and then by the French. Throughout that time the people of Vietnam were learning new culinary methods and techniques.

As you peruse a Vietnamese menu you will witness those influences through the use of everything from lemongrass and curry paste to croissants and baguettes. Naturally, the Asian staple starch appears as a major item. Not only do you see rice served steamed as a side dish but it also appears in noodles and as rice paper for wrapping. Vietnamese foods have a delicate fresh taste and are never heavy in texture or flavor. Herbs are used as greens as well as for flavor. Dishes made with curry may be ordered spiced according to personal preference.

A Vietnamese meal is served family style where everyone samples each dish. Preparation is not a detailed or complicated endeavor but rather is a gathering of fresh healthful ingredients handled and cooked as little as possible. A favorite example is the banh hoi. This popular dish is made by taking grilled marinated meat slices and placing them onto a rice paper wrapper piled with pickled daikon and carrots, bean sprouts, romaine, rice vermicelli, and fresh mint leaves. This is then rolled up like a burrito and dipped into a light, flavorful sauce.

Vietnamese cuisine is the new kid on Hawaii's culinary block. Although some of the surroundings may be a little basic, go in and try this wonderful taste experience just once and you will find yourself wanting to go back for more!

LOCAL FOOD

Local food is the Hawaiian Everyman's version of homegrown comfort food. Its roots go back to the plantation days when people were recruited from around the world to work the sugar cane and pineapple fields. Although they lived in separate camps the workers gathered in small groups for lunch and that is where the blending of cultures began.

The field workers' diet was pretty simple. Just about everyone had a tin of rice and some kind of meat and vegetable. A Japanese worker might bring some teriyaki beef and his Portuguese comrade might have a can of sardines. The Koreans would certainly bring along some kim chee and the Filipinos their adobo and lumpia. Then in a kind of Hawaiian potluck the workers would share what they brought bringing variety to an otherwise ordinary lunch in the field.

That was the beginning of local food, but what does it look like today? When you think local food think of something simple a plantation family would keep in their pantry. First comes the staple starch, which is nearly always rice. Then you have canned meat of which Spam, Vienna Sausages, sardines, corned beef, and beef stew predominate. To add a little interest there would be a jar of mayonnaise and a bag of macaroni with which to make a simple mac salad. Then the upcountry farmers would bring down their cabbage and dinner would be served.

Most visitors to Hawaii experience local food at one of the diners that can be found just about everywhere in the islands. The standard offering is what is commonly called a plate lunch. For six or seven dollars you get a choice of meat such as teri chicken, katsu pork, or mahi mahi, "two scoop" rice, and a scoop of mac salad. The whole affair comes appropriately served in a Styrofoam carryout container complete with plastic table service. Bon Appetit!

Now if a big bowl of noodle soup is more your style, local food can accommodate you as well. The staple item here is known as saimin. The history of this dish is interesting. The Chinese say it has a Japanese origin and the Japanese say it came from China, so they both must be right! To make saimin, first you must have a stock. In the Japanese tradition this would be a dashi which is a broth made from nori flavored with bonito shavings. Since this is a little lean for many tastes the choices take off from there. Some places use a chicken stock and others a beef broth. Determining your preference and figuring out who is using what is part of the adventure of exploring the local food establishments.

Then come the noodles that by tradition are made from wheat flour, eggs, and water. This "long rice" is complemented with a little meat and perhaps an egg as well as some Chinese cabbage to top the whole thing off. Local diners will buy a teri beef stick or two to add flavor to their bowl or to eat along side with some hot mustard. Make sure you try adding a dash of hot sauce for added zest.

PACIFIC RIM CUISINE

In a geographical sense Pacific Rim refers to all of the nations that border the Pacific Ocean. This area not only includes Japan, Korea, China, and Southeast Asia but it also takes in Australia, New Zealand, and all of Polynesia as well as South, Central, and North America. However, no matter how large that seems physically, in a cultural sense the Pacific Rim involves even that much more.

People from diverse cultures have shared their culinary traditions since the beginning of time. This interaction has greatly accelerated as global commercial activity, improved communications, and personal travel experiences impacted the general public. During the 20th century our new awareness of different culinary tastes and practices began to change people's expectations regardless of where they stood on the economic ladder. Witness the evolving trends of American dietary culture as we went from Italian and Chinese to Mexican and Thai. Once we began to sample exciting new flavors we didn't want to stop.

This brings us to a better understanding of the dynamics behind the Pacific Rim movement. Watching the explosion of mass-produced ethnic convenience foods, what enterprising young chef wouldn't try to capitalize on a new trend? Taking advantage of opportunity, professional chefs began using their classic training to blend ingredients from one group of countries and cooking methods from another to produce results that are on a higher level than the sum of the parts.

For instance, grilled beef tenderloin with shiitake mushrooms in a Marsala demi glace served with mashed Hawaiian taro and Okinawan sweet potatoes is a far cry from a grilled steak and baked potato. The combination uses Chinese, French, Italian, Hawaiian, Okinawan, Continental European and American foods and methods to elevate the diner's experience. The chef's education and experience in blending flavors led to the resulting balanced and pleasing entree.

In the Hawaiian Islands visitors sometimes wonder if they are experiencing Pacific Rim or Hawaii Regional Cuisine. Hawaii Regional Cuisine showcases locally produced fish, meats, fruits, and vegetables combined with local ethnic styles and classic cooking techniques to produce an upscale contemporary version of Hawaiian "local food". Pacific Rim Cuisine draws upon a much broader geographic area when sourcing its ingredients and cooking methods and ends up as an innovative fusion of cuisines from all around the Pacific Rim.

A visit to a Pacific Rim restaurant is like a visit to a foodie theme park. As you read the menu, try and picture the ingredients and tastes the chef is combining before you make your selection. Not all the world's tastes and textures are to everyone's liking. By thinking about what you really enjoy and then following your own lead you will be much better prepared to select those dishes more likely to please and experience a truly enjoyable dining experience.

HAWAII REGIONAL CUISINE

There was a time when dining in Hawaii was less than a stellar experience. Much of what appeared on restaurant menus had to be shipped in over long distances. Things that could be arrived frozen and those that couldn't arrived tired. Then, in an attempt to please the visitors, the local chefs tried to prepare classic cuisine under less than ideal circumstances. As you can imagine, cooking Continental out of a can didn't work very well.

Along came the late '80's and a group of young chefs decided that something had to be done to change the situation. They began to talk with local farmers, fishermen, and ranchers about the types of products needed to raise the level of their culinary offerings. Then, in order to create new and exciting dishes, these chefs began merging local cultural influences with their newfound sources of supply and Hawaii Regional Cuisine was on its way to being born

In the original group there were twelve chefs who banded together and formally created the Hawaii Regional Cuisine movement. Those twelve are: Sam Choy, Roger Dikon, Mark Ellman, Bev Gannon, Jean Marie Josselin, George Mavrothalassitis (Mavro), Peter Merriman, Amy Ferguson Ota, Philippe Padovani, Gary Strehl, Alan Wong, and Roy Yamaguchi. Their goal was to combine fresh island products with local ethnic cooking styles and classic techniques in a contemporary upscale regional cuisine unique to Hawaii.

Hawaii Regional Cuisine is a fusion of elements from both eastern and western cultures. Much of the inspiration comes from the meager beginnings of the plantation camps and what islanders call "local food". Add that to an innovative group of classically trained chefs and the freshest of local products and you get truly unique preparations unlike anything you've ever experienced.

There are an amazing variety of offerings on a Hawaii Regional Cuisine menu. Naturally, fresh island fish like opakapaka and mahi-mahi appear regularly, but so do local aquaculture products like Kahuku prawns and Keahole lobster. Look for the Asian preparations and Polynesian sauces that take these specialties one-step beyond. Then to complement the seafood dishes, you might find innovative items like pineapple chicken or macadamia crusted lamb rounding things out.

While you are traveling in the islands keep an eye out for restaurants operated by any of the twelve original Hawaii Regional Cuisine chefs. They will surely provide you with a memorable evening of dining enjoyment. There is also a new group of young up and coming chefs who are doing wonderful work in Hawaii. These people call themselves the Hawaiian Island Chefs and include Steven Ariel, Chai Chaowasaree, Hiroshi Fukui, Teresa Gannon, George Gomes, Wayne Hirabayashi, D. K. Kodama, Lance Kosaka, Jacqueline Lau, Douglas Lum, James McDonald, Mark Okumura, Russell Siu, Goren Streng, and Corey Waite. Look for them. They are the new wave and they're here today.

Legend

Dress Code and Restaurant Price Symbols are based upon dinner. Lunch is usually a less expensive meal with more casual attire acceptable.

Restaurant Prices:

$	<$10
$$	$10-25
$$$	$25-$40
$$$$	$40+
Ent Card	Entertainment Card

The Entertainment Card travel discount card offers sizeable discounts and may be purchased for many geographic areas. You can view the benefits and order a directory and card at www.entertainment.com. At this writing the cost for the Hawaii package is $35.00. Fine, moderate, and casual dining choices are offered at many locations in Hawaii but are most common on Oahu. These books are released in limited quantities every November and do sell out. Either order early online or ask at your local bookstore. Make sure that you get the membership card with your copy. It should be attached inside the front cover.

Credit Cards Accepted:

AE	American Express
CB	Carte Blanche
DC	Diners Club
DIS	Discover
JCB	Japan Credit Bank
MC	Master Card
V	Visa

Days of Operation:

Su	Sunday
Mo	Monday
Tu	Tuesday
We	Wednesday
Th	Thursday
Fr	Friday
Sa	Saturday
X	Except

Example: XMo=Every Day Except Monday

Service Code:

Bru=Brunch   **Buf**-Buffet

Cuisine Code:

Amer	American
Asian	Asian
Car	Caribbean
Chi	Chinese
Cof	Coffee
Cont	Continental
Ec	Eclectic
Euro	European
Fili	Filipino
Fre	French
Ger	German
Grk	Greek
Haw-Reg	Hawaiian Regional
Haw	Hawaiian
Ind	Indian
Indo	Indonesian
Isl	Island
Ital	Italian
Japan	Japan
Kor	Korean
Local	Local
LatAm	Latin American
Med	Mediterranean
Mex	Mexican
Org	Organic
Pac	Pacific
Pac-Rim	Pacific Rim
Port	Portuguese
Sea	Seafood
Spec	Specialty
Stk	Steak
Thai	Thailand
Trop	Tropical
Veg	Vegetarian
Viet	Vietnamese

Dress Code:

Casual	sandals, t shirts, shorts
Resort Casual	shirt with a collar, shorts with pockets, no flip-flops
Evening Aloha	long pants on gentlemen with closed-toed shoes
Formal	long sleeved dress shirt or jacket for gentlemen; inquire
Note:	Bathing suits and tank tops are suitable attire on the beach and by the pool. Cover-ups are an absolute must at even the most casual of dining spots.

Menu Items:

Nothing in the world of travel changes faster than restaurant menus. Everything from the seasonal availability of produce to which side of the bed the chef got up on impacts what you're offered when you sit down to dine. Nowhere is this more true than in Hawaii where the catch of the day really is caught that day. If the boats didn't bring opakapaka in, it just isn't available.

This guide attempts to help the reader come to his own conclusions. Menu items were chosen to give a well-rounded cross-section of the offerings and a sense of their depth and complexity. Signature dishes have been included whenever possible as they tend to be constants and best represent the expertise and direction of the chef. Finally, prices are always subject to change and should be viewed as guidelines of affordability.

Reservations:

It is always wise to call ahead. Even the most notable restaurants change their hours and days of operation. This is particularly true in travel destinations like Hawaii where business tends to be seasonal.

Spelling & Punctuation:

We have attempted to duplicate the spelling and punctuation as they appear on individual menus. If you think that some of them are unusual, you should have seen what they did to our spell check and grammar programs!

27

Kauai

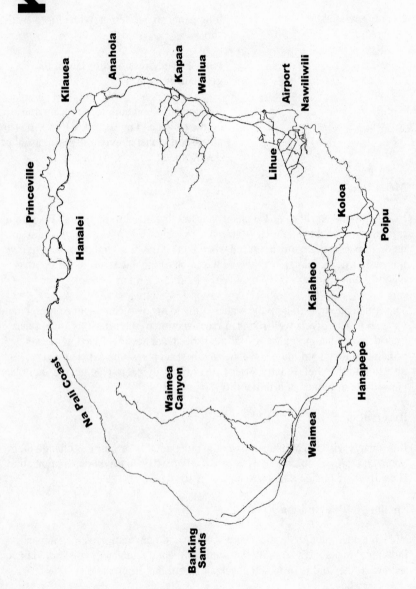

N E S W

Princeville

Kilauea

Anahola

Kapaa

Wailua

Airport

Nawiliwili

Lihue

Hanalei

Koloa

Poipu

Kalaheo

Na Pali Coast

Waimea
Canyon

Hanapepe

Waimea

Barking
Sands

KAUAI DINING

Lihue

Aromas
Harbor Mall
3501 Rice Street-Suite 207
Lihue, HI 96766
808-245-9192
Web: None
Hours: B 8:00 AM-11:30 AM XMoTuWe
         L 11:30 AM-4:30 PM XMoTuWe
         D 5:00 PM-9:30 PM XMo
Cards: AE DIS JCB MC V
Dress: Resort Casual
Style: Ecl/Med/PacRim $$

Menu Sampler:

Breakfast:
French Toast of Portuguese sweet bread dipped in vanilla, orange & cinnamon batter w/coconut or maple syrup $6.50, Kauai Crown Fried Rice & Eggs, guava toast points $7.25, Aromas Omelette w/potatoes/rice & toast $6.95-$8.25

Lunch:
Salads: Aegean Salad w/feta cheese, cucumbers, red onions, tomatoes, carrots, garbanzo beans, mixed greens, Kalamata olives, roasted red peppers $9.95
Entrees: Firehouse Chinese Chicken Salad w/crispy chow mein noodles and caramelized almonds $9.95, Kuhio Hwy Steak Wrap, onions, peppers, w/horseradish poppy seed spread rolled in a chipotle chili wrap $9.95

Dinner:
Appetizers: Coconut, Ginger, Carrot Bisque topped with a green onion & shrimp ratia $7.50, Thai Vegetable Summer Roll w/sweet chili & peanut $7.75
Entrees: Grilled New York Steak topped w/honey & sweet onions, gorgonzola cheese and a cabernet sauvignon demi glaze $24.95, Twisted Sister Mahi Mahi-honey and pecan crusted Mahi Mahi with twisted prawns in a coconut & mint orange beurre blanc $23.95, Crepes Kainoa stuffed w/roasted chicken, red peppers, white corn, shallots, smoked gouda cheese & roasted garlic herb $14.95

Impressions:

We particularly like chef-owned and operated dining venues, as they provide the perfect stage for culinary self-expression. This scenario plays well at Aroma's where the ambitious menu comes with bold accents and varied choices. Robert Moler has created this little gem on the second floor of the Harbor Mall complex overlooking Nawiliwili Bay just south of Lihue. Reservations are recommended.

Kauai Dining

North Shore

Bali Hai
Hanalei Bay Resort
5380 Honoiki Road
Princeville, HI 96722
808-826-6522
www.hanaleibayresort.com

Hours: B 7:00 AM-11:00 AM
          L 11:30 AM-2:00 PM
          D 5:30 PM-9:00 PM
Cards: AE DIS MC V
Dress: Resort Casual
Style: Haw-Reg/Pac-Rim $$

Menu Sampler:

Breakfast:
Traditional and island favorites such as Garden Island Omelet $10.50, Poi Pancakes $8.25, Seafood Omelet $13.50, Breakfast Burritos $8.25
Lunch: Kauai Onion Soup with melted provolone $4.95, Kauai Avocado and Vegi Pita served with hummus and cucumber dill sour cream $9.95, Quiche of the Day served with tropical fruit compote and garden salad $14.95
Dinner:
First Courses: Bali Hai Crabcakes served on roasted Kauai sweet corn with curry butter sauce & mango-papaya relish $12.75, Ahi Poke Tower $12.75, Namalokama beef and chicken sate platter $14.50
Entrées: Marinated Grilled Lamb Chops with mushroom risotto, garlic and rosemary demi glace $30.95, Fresh Catch prepared "Tropical Breeze" sautéed with a cool papaya and pineapple salsa, wasabi garlic mashed potatoes $27 or as "Rock Jumping Fisherman" broiled, topped with green coconut milk, sweet chili & peanut sate sauce $27, Makai Lobster pasta medley, ½ grilled lobster, sautéed shrimp and scallops finished with a brandy cream sauce $36.95

Impressions:

Perched high on a ridge overlooking the famed Bali Hai setting from the movie "South Pacific" there's a beautiful restaurant where romantic Hawaii still lives. . Appropriately every table enjoys a stunning panoramic view of the bay and the mountains beyond. The kitchen keeps pace with the surroundings serving up innovative preparations combining ingredients and techniques from around the Pacific. Those on a budget will find the breakfast and lunch menus a welcome alternative. This is a very romantic dining spot regardless of time of day..

Kauai Dining

North Shore

Bamboo Bamboo
Hanalei Center
Kuhio Hwy
Hanalei, HI 96714
Phone: 808-826-1177
Web: None
Hours: L 11:30 AM-2:30 PM XMo
        D 5:30 PM-9:30 PM
Cards: AE JCB MC V
Dress: Resort Casual
Style: Cont/Pac-Rim $$$

Menu Sampler:

Breakfast:
N/A
Lunch:
Hanalei Taro Burger with lettuce, tomato, onion $8.95, Fish & Chips
w/seasoned fries $10.95, Chicken Pesto Sandwich on sourdough $8.95
Dinner:
Appetizers: Fresh Vegetable Summer Rolls w/sweet chili sauce $8.95, Kilauea
Crispy Ahi Spring Rolls with wasabi cream sauce $9.95, Calamari Fritters with
papaya cocktail sauce $8.95, Shrimp Cocktail $9.50, Summer Rolls $8.95
Pasta:
Entrées: Brick Oven Pizza-Margharita-white pie of garlic olive oil spread,
sliced tomato, fresh basil topped with parmesan and mozzarella cheese $16.95,
Potato Crusted Mahi Mahi or Ono served in a beurre rouge wine sauce with
steamed rice $25.95, North Shore Seafood Pasta in white wine, garlic, and herbs
topped with a marinara $23.95, Gina's Filet Mignon, 8 oz. grilled, served with
sautéed mushrooms and garlic mashed potatoes $28.95, Haena Shrimp-six
macadamia nut crusted shrimp in a sweet Thai chili sauce, rice $22.95
Desserts: Tiramisu $7.00, Apple Pie a la Mode $5.50

Impressions:

Near the end of the road in the quaint village of Hanalei travelers will find a
comfortable chef-owned restaurant known as Bamboo Bamboo. The spacious
indoor/outdoor dining area has a Pacific/Indonesian décor and features original
artwork on the walls. The innovative menu offers a little something for everyone
including pizza for the kids. The fine food is backed by a substantial wine list
and a full service bar. Espresso and Cappuccino fans come right this way!

South Shore

Beach House
5022 Lawai Road
Koloa, HI 96756
808-742-1424
www.the-beach-house.com
Hours: 5:30 PM-10:00 PM
Cards: AE DC MC V
Dress: Resort Casual
Style: Pac-Rim $$$

Menu Sampler:

Breakfast/Lunch:
N/A
Dinner:
Appetizers: Thai Curry Shrimp & Scallop Wonton, mango Thai basil, mint cucumber sauce 12, Shiitake Crusted Mussels, black bean sauce, ginger lime beurre blanc 9, Fish Nachos, refried black Thai rice, roasted corn/Hawaiian 12, Togarashi Fried Calamari w/guava sauce 9
Soup and Salad: Omoa Baby Lettuce, roasted sesame orange vinaigrette 7, Seafood Corn Chowder with fresh thyme and sherry 8, Blackened Ahi Caesar, romaine lettuce, feta & parmesan cheese, herb croutons 12
Entrées: Chinese Style Roasted Duck, lemon orange Grand Marnier demi, shiitake risotto cake, pickled vegetables, pesto 26, Porcini Dusted Hamachi, Seared Scallops, Edamame Risotto, Tomato Ginger Truffle Coulis 29, Filet Mignon, peppered sweet onion, au gratin potato, red wine demi-glaze 29, Wasabi Crusted Snapper, lilikoi lemon grass beurre blanc 29
Desserts: Beach House Tiramisu 6.50, Bananas Foster 6.50, Molten Chocolate Desire (allow 20 minutes for preparation)

Impressions:

The Beach House has one of the most dramatic settings you'll find in Hawaii. Outside, there's the Pacific Ocean splashing up on the rocks. Inside, diners find fine Pacific Rim cuisine served in a casual yet upscale atmosphere. The menu has been broadened recently and offers a nice variety of enticing selections. This special dining spot is very busy so be sure to make reservations. Valet parking is almost a must as there is no lot on the premises and space is very limited in the surrounding area. Pupu and cocktail service begins at 5 PM so stop in early and secure your seat for the fabulous sunset viewing.

Kauai Dining

East Coast

Blossoming Lotus
4504 Kukui St
Kapa'a, HI 96746
808-822-7678
www.blossominglotus.com
Hours: L 11:00 AM-3:00 PM Mo-Fr
       Bru 11:00 AM-3:00 PM SaSu
       D 5:30 PM-9:30 PM
Cards: MC V
Dress: Resort Casual
Style: Org $$

Menu Sampler:

Breakfast:
N/A
Lunch:
Wraps & Sandwiches: J-Love's Grilled Veggie Sandwich of marinated & grilled seasonal veggies, grilled onion, lettuce, sprouts, basil-katook pesto on homemade spelt bread $9, Menehune's Maki Roll of brown rice, assorted veggies, spicy tuna spread wrapped in a nori sheet with sprouts, green onion and served with wasabi, pickled ginger and a shoyu dipping sauce $6
Salads: Aiyah's Garden of Eden Salad-island organic mixed greens, sprouts, fresh veggies and choice of two of the following: purple potato salad, tuna free tempeh salad, hummus du jour or our live food pate $15
Dinner:
Appetizers: Pizanno's Pizettas-rosemary masa crust pizzas with herbed cashew-pine nut cheese, alii mushrooms, tomatoes, basil & garlic 11
Sunny Sides of Life: Kalalau's Green Papaya Salad with fresh cilantro in a live Thai lime sauce served with marinated lotus root & starfruit $5
Entrées: Rama's Red Curry-Okinawan purple sweet potato in a red coconut curry sauce w/leeks and fresh vegetables served over brown rice or quinoa $10

Impressions:

Blossoming Lotus is one of the select few vegetarian restaurants that have successfully made the leap from niche to mainstream. Their talented chef has received recognition for his vegan world fusion cuisine. During a recent visit we had to pass on lunch, as they were taping a show in the kitchen! Places of this type tend to occupy space that is as alternative as their menus. Not so with this one. They recently moved into new digs that are as artistic as the preparations.

South Shore

Brennecke's Beach Broiler
2100 Hoone Road
Koloa, HI 96756
808-742-7588
www.brenneckes.com
Hours: LD 11:00 AM-10:00 PM
Cards: AE DC DIS MC V
Dress: Resort Casual
Style: Sea/Stk $$$

Menu Sampler:

Breakfast:
N/A

Lunch:
Pupus: Ceviche 9.95, Seared Ahi 12.95, BBQ Baby Back Ribs 15.95, Nachos with cheese and peppers 9.95, Shrimp Cocktail 10.95, Chicken Skewers 8.50, Sashimi of Ahi 12.95, Shrimp Stuffed Mushrooms 12.95, Oriental Pupu Sampler 13.95, NY Steak 'N Mushrooms 19.75, Kama Aina Pupu Favorites 15.95
Soups, Salads, Sandwiches: Fresh Fish Sandwich 11.95, Prime Rib Sandwich 12.95, NE Style Clam Chowder 3.25/4.95, Ahi Caesar Salad 13.95, Soup, Salad Bar, Bread Combo 11.95, Fresh Ahi Wrap 12.95, Brennecke's Beach Burger Deluxe 9.95, Chicken Teriyaki Sandwich 10.95, Vegetarian Burger 9.95
Dinner: all entrees served with choice of salad bar or chowder; sautéed vegetables, steamed rice or herb pasta and dinner roll. Fresh Island Fish-kiawe broiled or sautéed with white wine, garlic and butter 25.50, Brennecke's Special Scampi 25.95, 10 oz. New York with Mushrooms 25.50, Baby Back Pork BBQ Ribs 24.50, Cioppino 26.50, Prime Rib 20.50/23.50/25.50, Fresh Seafood Kebab 24.50, Hawaiian Spiny Lobster Tail $Mkt, Alaskan King Crab Legs $Mkt., Fresh Vegetables Sautéed in wine, garlic cream sauce on a bed of pasta 19.95
Brennecke's Happy Hour: 3:00 PM-5:00 PM; Mai Tai 4.25, Tall Margarita on the Rocks 4.25, Shrimp & Fries 8.95, Calamari & Fries 8.95, Hot Wings 8.95

Impressions:

First time visitors to this place might get the impression that they are in south Florida instead of Hawaii. The flat-roofed two-story building would be just as much at home on Key Largo as in Poipu Beach. Same holds for the menu. You won't get fusion confusion in this establishment. Instead, mainstream steak and seafood are the specialty of the house. Recent upgrades to all aspects of their operation make this a solid casual dining choice.

West Side

Brick Oven Pizza

2-2555 Kaumualii Hwy (Hwy 50)
Kalaheo, HI 96741
808-332-8561
Web: None
Hours: L/D 11:00 AM-10:00 PM XMo
Cards: MC V
Dress: Casual
Style: Ital $

Authors' Favorite

Menu Sampler:

Breakfast:
N/A

Lunch/Dinner:
Pizza: Hearth Baked Pizzas made of whole wheat or white crust brushed with garlic butter $9.95-$29.35 in 10", 12", 15" sizes, Pizza Bread (one slice) $2.95 w/traditional ingredients such as Italian sausage (they make their own), salami, pepperoni, black olives, mushrooms, anchovies, or Seafood Style Pizza Bread w/bay shrimp, cheddar cheese, green onions, pizza sauce or garlic butter $3.40
Sandwiches: Hot Super Sandwich of smoked ham, salami, pepperoni, cheese, mustard, lettuce, tomatoes, onions $6.95, Italian Sausage Sandwich of homemade Italian sausage, pizza sauce, cheese, lettuce, tomatoes, white onions $7.15, Garlic Toast $.75/slice, with cheese $1.30/slice, Roast Beef Sandwich-au jus, white onion $7.25, Open Face of smoked ham, tomato, provolone cheese $7.40, Chicken Sandwich with Italian seasonings, mayo, onion $6.95
Salads: Veggie Salad of greens, zucchini, mushrooms, bell pepper, black olives, onions, mozzarella and cheddar cheese in small $3.95 or large $5.95
Desserts: Aloha Pie $2.85, Chocolate/Strawberry Sundae Ice Cream Cups $.80

Impressions:

The village of Kalaheo is just a short distance from Poipu and Koloa. As you enter town from the north you'll see Brick Oven Pizza mauka of the highway. Here you'll find one of the best pizzas in Hawaii. The garlic butter-brushed crust is excellent and comes with a large variety of traditional toppings. Vegetarians will like the sauce as it's made without meat or poultry stock. Everybody will like the 100% real mozzarella cheese! Brick Oven Pizza is family owned and has been offering good food at reasonable prices since 1970. In keeping with Italian tradition, wine and beer are available.

North Shore

Café Hanalei
Princeville Hotel
5520 Ka Haku Road
Princeville, HI 96722
808-826-2760
www.princeville.com
Hours: Su Bru 10:00 AM-2:00 PM
        B 6:30 AM-11:00 AM XSu
        L 11:00 AM-2:30 PM XSu
        D 5:30 PM-9:30 PM
Cards: AE JCB MC V
Dress: Resort Casual
Style: Pac-Rim $$$

Menu Sampler:

Breakfast:
Sunday Brunch: 10 AM-2 PM. $42.00 with champagne. Buffet of a wide variety of exotic salads, seafood, pastas, carved meats, breakfast classics
Daily Breakfast: Breakfast buffet $23.95, Continental Breakfast $17.50, Japanese Breakfast $24.95/$19.95, Hanalei Taro Pancakes-apple bananas $11.50
Lunch:
Hawaiian style Chicken Salad w/sweet potato hash, organic greens & crispy tofu $15.95, Grilled Fresh Albacore sandwich w/sesame miso aioli & pickled vegetables $15.95, Passionfruit Mousse with Kula Strawberries $6.50
Dinner:
Appetizers: Hanalei Seafood Chowder with taro, luau leaf, coconut milk 8.00, Kalua Duck Lumpia with poha-ume dipping sauce, lomi tomato relish 16.00
Entrées: Mochiko Chicken stuffed with long rice and shiitake mushrooms, served with mochi rice risotto, citrus soy reduction, and mustard soy drizzle 29.00, Lemon Grass Crusted Ahi with shrimp dumplings 34.00
Dessert: Rum Roasted Pineapple served warm with coconut ice cream 7.00, Hawaiian Vanilla Bean Crème Brulee with macadamia nut biscotti 7.00
Friday Night Seafood Buffet: 5:30-9:30 PM $49.95/adults, $3.50/year - children. Salads, cold and hot seafood, carved items, wok station
.

Impressions:

This decidedly upscale restaurant is located in one of the most beautiful hotels in the islands. The fabulous setting high on a ridge overlooking Bali Hai is as good as it gets. The menu at Café Hanalei is quite ambitious and doesn't disappoint. Stop by the Princeville Resort and let the North Shore work it's magic!

Lihue

Café Portofino   **Authors' Favorite**
Kauai Marriott Resort
3610 Rice Street
Nawiliwili, HI 96766
808-245-2121
www.cafeportofino.com
Hours: D 5:00 PM-10:00 PM
Cards: AE DC DIS MC V
Dress: Resort Casual
Style: Ital $$$

Menu Sampler:

Breakfast/Lunch:
N/A
Dinner:
Antipasti: Escargot Maison 10.00, Calamari Fritti 10.00, Mozzarella Marinara 9.00, Pepperoni Arrostiti 10.00, Steamed Clams $Market Price
Zuppe: Minestrone alla Portofino-mixed fresh vegetables with garlic and oregano 6.50, Gaspacio-cold spiced fresh tomato soup 6.50, Soup of the Day
Pasta: Penne Broccoli Spinach 16.00, Fettuccine Alfredo 16.50, Linguine a la Carbonara 17.00, Fettuccine Shrimp & Mushroom in a creamy sauce 24.00
Insalate: Caesar Salad 8.00, Green Salad with house dressing 7.00
Specialite d'ella Casa: Osso Buco alla Portofino-veal shank in a traditional sauce on a bed of fettucine 29.00, Scampi a la Limone 24.00, Melanzane a la Parmigiana 18.00, Scampi alla Provinciale w/butter, white wine, garlic 24.00
Secondi di Vitello: Scaloppine alla Parmigiana-medallions of veal in tomato sauce with mozzarella cheese 26.00, Scaloppine a la Piccata or Marsala 26.00, Scaloppine alla Portofino with lemon-sage butter sauce 26.00
D'Alla Griglia: Chicken Cacciatore 20.00, Pollo Porcini-chicken breast sautéed, and flambé in brandy with a light wild mushroom sauce 24.00
Daily specials are posted.

Impressions:

This romantic white linen and black tie restaurant recently relocated to new digs next to Duke's Kauai on Kalapaki Beach. The specialty of the house is Northern Italian cuisine, and you'll have to look hard to find better. Whether choosing to dine indoors or out, customers are treated to a gracious continental experience with tropical flair. This is one of our favorite dining experiences on the island.

South Shore

Casablanca at Kiahuna
Kiahuna Tennis Club
2290 Poipu Road
Poipu, HI 96756
808-262-8196
Web: None
Hours: B 7:30 AM-11 AM Mo-Sa
        B 8:30 AM-Noon Su
        L 11:30 AM-3:00 PM Mo-Sa
        L Noon-3:00 PM Su
        D 6:00 PM-9:00 PM Tu-Sa
Cards: DC DIS MC V
Dress: Resort Casual
Style: Med $$$

Menu Sampler:

Breakfast:
Waffles with fresh fruit or macadamia nuts 8, Omelette du Jour 8, Eggs Benedict 9, Eggs Florentine 9, French Toast of Challah with fruit 9
Lunch:
Salads: Spinach with a roasted garlic-Dijon vinaigrette, pancetta, pine nuts $10
Entrees: Panini of mozzarella, prosciutto, onions, or grilled vegetables 8, Casa Pita Plate with grilled lamb, mint yogurt dressing, spicy harissa $12
Dinner:
Entrees: Crispy Seared Duck Breast flavored with a balsamic glaze of capers and garlic, served with mashed root vegetables $19, Ribeye Steak dry-rubbed with sugar & salt, seasoned with porcini mushroom powder, red pepper flakes and garlic, drizzled with a balsamic vinegar reduction, roasted potatoes $26, Spanish seafood stew of lobster, shrimp, scallops, calamari and mussels in a savory broth $28, Penne tossed with a light brandy cream sauce $14
Tapas: served Su Noon-3 PM, Mo-Sa 11:30 AM-6:00 PM
Eggplant Caponata Agrodolce with raisins, olives, capers and pine nuts $5, Moroccan B'Steeya Crepe-chicken, cinnamon, saffron and almonds $7

Impressions:

Centered in the Kiahuna resort's pool and tennis club complex there's a jewel of a restaurant serving exciting tastes from the Mediterranean. Throughout the day visitors to Casablanca can enjoy a step away from the ordinary. This is alfresco dining where bold tastes rule and the timid need not apply.

South Shore

Casa di Amici   **Authors' Favorite**
2301 Nalo Road
Poipu, HI 96756
808-742-1555
Web: None
Hours: D 6:00 PM-Closing
Cards: DC MC V
Dress: Resort Casual
Style: Itai/Sea/Cont $$$

Menu Sampler:

Breakfast/Lunch:
N/A
Dinner:
Pupus: Gnocchi Quatro Formaggio with four cheese filling with a tomato-sage-pancetta sauce gratineed with Grana Padano Parmesan $8, Calamari Fritte breaded in Panko Flakes in a piccatta sauce $8, Chesapeake Bay style crab cakes with a passion fruit lobster sauce $9, Chili Verde Risotto with tortillas $9
Salades: Insalata Di Pomodoro of sliced tomatoes, sweet red onions, fresh mozzarella, olive tapenade, and fresh basil with a raspberry vinaigrette $8, Caesar w/croutons $6, Fresh Romaine with creamy basil-tarragon vinaigrette $5
Pasta: Fettucine Alfredo $17, Scampi Di Amici w/garlic-linguine $23, Shrimp Half-Moon Ravioli w/black tiger prawns, saffron-orange lobster sauce $19
Entrée: Tournedos Rossini-sauteed medallions of filet finished in a Madeira-shallot sauce, served with an Asian spiced pate, fluted mushroom caps atop garlic croutons $24, Veal Piccatta of sautéed veal scaloppini finished in a chardonnay lemon-caper sauce-light $18/regular $23, Duck Confit $18.00/23.00, Lobster Tails in a white truffle sauce with fresh carrots, zucchini, tomato, and peas served on farfalle $26, Japanese Mahogany Glazed Salmon and Grilled Black Tiger Prawns served on black frijoles chonitos $25
Desserts: Bananas Foster serves two $7, Tiramisu $7

Impressions:

This intimate dining spot is located in a residential neighborhood behind Poipu Beach. Casa di Amici features upscale Italian fare with Pacific Rim touches on their ambitious, well-executed menu. The combination adds an exotic spin to the preparations. Reservations are a must at this romantic little restaurant. Parking in the lot is limited and on the street nearly impossible, so we suggest dining early.

East Coast

Coconuts Island Style Grill & Bar   Authors' Favorite
4-919 Kuhio Highway
Kapa'a, HI 96746
808-823-8777
Web: None
Hours: D 4:00 PM-10:00 PM XSu
Cards: AE DC JCB MC V
Dress: Resort Casual
Style: Pac Rim/Trop $$$

Menu Sampler:

Breakfast/Lunch:
N/A
Dinner:
Pupus: Lobster Ravioli with saffron sauce & two tobiko $9.50, Coconut
Seafood Cigars served with sweet pineapple chili chutney $7.95, Dragon Fire
Baby Back Ribs served with a cooling slaw & sesame-citrus dressing $9.95
Salads: Kapa'a Organic Greens with balsamic dressing, candied pecans &
Gorgonzola cheese $6.75, Goat Cheese & Organic Garden Greens $8.50,
Coconut's Sautéed Scallop Salad, mac nuts, lime-coconut dressing $11.50
Main Things: Big Crispy Veal Scaloppine with balsamic basil sauce, capellini
& veggies $19.95, Grilled & Teriyaki Dipped Salmon with lilikoi ponzu sauce,
coconut scallion rice, cucumber salad & veggies $16.50, Tempura Dipped Ono
served with ginger wasabi aioli, stir fried rice & veggies $20.95, Seafood Paella
w/shrimp, scallops, mussels, calamari, saffron rice & veggies $19.75, Coconuts
Special Sirloin Steak w/red zinfandel sauce, veggies, twice baked or garlic
gratin potato $24.95, Crispy Chicken breast & garlic mashed potato $16.95
Desserts: Classic Crème Brulee topped w/caramelized bananas & raspberry
sauce $5.75, Pineapple Upside Down Cake w/coconut sorbet & mango coulis
$5.75, Chocolate Volcano Cake served warm with Kona Coffee Sauce $5.75

Impressions:

What a fun, lively place! The tropical décor and innovative cuisine at Coconut's
really packs them in. Get there early to put your name in for a table as they only
take reservations for parties of six or more. Then let your imagination take over
as you graze some of the best pupus found on Kauai. Don't overdo it though as
you'll want to follow through with one of their innovative entrées. Of course, no
meal would be complete without dessert and once again, Coconut's shines.

South Shore

Dali Deli
5492 Koloa Road
Koloa, HI 96756
808-742-8824
Web: None
Hours: B/L 8:00 AM-3:00 PM Mo-Sa
Cards: AE MC V
Dress: Casual
Style: Amer $

Menu Sampler:

Breakfast:
Two Eggs with ham, bacon, or sausage and home fries, toast or a bagel $6.95, French Toast made with challah bread and served with fresh island fruit $6.95, Breakfast Burrito with a spinach tortilla filled with scrambled eggs, refried beans, green chilies, sautéed onions and sour cream, topped with cheddar cheese and fresh salsa $7.95, Daily Dali Omelet with home fries, toast or a bagel $7.95, Pancakes (3) with fresh island fruit $6.95, Bacon & Cheese Bagelwich $7.95

Lunch:
Daily Soup $3.25/$5.75, Italian Sub on a French Roll with balsamic vinaigrette $7.25, Grilled Marinated Portobello Mushroom Sandwich with garlic mayo on a French roll with a choice of salad, fries $8.75, Cajun Shrimp Sandwich with red bell peppers, lettuce and Creole spices & garlic mayo on a French Roll $9.25, Meat Loaf Sandwich on a grilled French roll with salad or fries $7.95, Philly Cheese Steak with salad or fries $7.95, Hello Dali of fresh roast turkey, cranberry relish, and lettuce on a French roll $7.25, Caprisce Sandwich of fresh mozzarella, pesto, arugula, tomato and lemon olive oil on a French roll $6.95, Greek Salad $5.95 with hummus $6.75, Daily Mystery Salad $???, Dali Daily Soup $3.25/$5.75, with salad $4.75/$7.25

Dinner:
N/A

Impressions:

At the quiet end of Koloa's main street there's a plantation style eatery whose simple exterior belies the goodies waiting inside. This is Dali Deli, where those looking for affordable, interesting tastes can find breakfast and lunch. Although the surroundings are simple, the approach is ambitious and well-executed. As an added treat, baked goods are offered along with lattes, cappuccino, and espresso. This casual restaurant is colorful, comfortable, and friendly.

Kauai Dining

South Shore

Dondero's
Hyatt Regency Kauai Resort & Spa
1571 Poipu Road
Koloa, HI 96756
808-742-6260
www.kauai.hyatt.com

Hours: D 6:00 PM-10:00 PM
Cards: AE DC DIS JCB MC V
Dress: Resort Casual
Style: Ital $$$$

Menu Sampler:

Breakfast/Lunch:
N/A

Dinner:
Appetizers: Carpaccio Dimanzo Con Rugula E Parmigiano of sliced lean tenderloin of beef, arugula, roasted pepper, shaved Parmesan cheese, and artichoke $15.50, Insalata Di Gorgonzola E Pomodori-tomato & Gorgonzola salad w/cracked black pepper, extra virgin olive oil, sweet basil $11.50
Pasta: Black Ink Fettucine with scallops, shrimps, mussels, salmon, clams, lobster, cognac bisque sauce, and black truffle $33.00, Lobster Picata with pistachio fettucine, sun dried tomato, truffle cream sauce $35.00
Entrée: Veal Loin Sautéed in Olive Oil with Parmesan cheese, fresh baby spinach, semolina cakes, porcini mushroom sauce $28.00, Roast Lamb Rack with herb crust, homemade gnocchi, asparagus, baby carrots, and lamb jus reduction $41.00, Grilled Beef Tenderloin on Mashed Eggplant, black truffle sauce and artichoke fritters $32.50, Chicken Parmigiana $27.00, Grilled Opakapaka w/roasted vegetables, tomatoes, olives, garlic, balsamic glaze $32.00
Desserts: Tiramisu $8.00, Amaretto Cheesecake & fresh berry sauce $8.50, Vanilla Crème Brulee with fresh berries $9.50, Fresh Fruit Sorbet $9.50

Impressions:

Dondero's offers a dining experience that's completely in step with its location in Poipu's benchmark resort. Just as The Hyatt Kauai Resort & Spa focuses on indulging oneself, their signature Italian restaurant can be counted on for an evening of superb fine dining. The perfect ending to a busy day begins when you are escorted into the elegantly appointed room or out onto the terrace. Then things move on to choices from an extensive wine list before choosing from the gourmet level Northern Italian menu. After dinner, remain at your table for a cognac, or retire to Stevenson's for an after dinner drink and a bit of live music.

North Shore

Duane's Ono-Char Burger
4-4350 Kuhio Hwy
Anahola, HI 96703
808-822-9181
Web: None
Hours: LD 10:00 AM-6:00 PM Mo-Sa
        LD 11:00 AM-4:00 PM Su
Cards: None
Dress: Casual
Style: Amer $

Menu Sampler:

Breakfast:
N/A
Lunch/Dinner:
Burgers: Ono (ono means delicious) Burger with lettuce and tomato-regular $4.15, Ono Cheeseburger $4.65, Old Fashioned Burger with cheddar, onion, sprouts, Kaiser roll $5.20, Teriyaki Burger (biggest seller)$4.70, BBQ Burger $4.70, Blue Cheese Burger $4.90, Avocado Burger $6.45, Local Boy Burger-teriyaki with cheddar and grilled pineapple $5.90, **Sandwiches:** Grilled Chicken $5.25, Patty Melt $4.95, Grilled Cheese $3.00, **Specialties:** Shrimp & Fries $7.75, Fish & Chips $3.65, $5.00, $6.50
Side Orders and Beverages: French Fries $1.20/$2.05, Onion Rings $2.50, Corn Dog $2.00, Ono's Tossed Green Salad $3.50, Papaya, Banana, Pineapple Juice & Crushed Ice $2.25/$2.50, Ice Cream Floats & Freezes $3.25

Impressions:

Duane's doesn't serve haute cuisine. This is a hamburger stand—nothing more, nothing less. Customers walk up to the window, place their orders, and wait to be called. As the name implies, the burgers are flame-grilled. They aren't overly large, but they come with a wild variety of toppings packed into a quality bun. Everything is served wrapped in paper ready to carry out or take over to the nearby picnic tables for a quick lunch. Those new to Duane's should note that there are no restroom facilities on site.

Lihue

Duke's Kauai
Kauai Marriott Resort
3610 Rice Street
Lihue, HI 96766
808-246-9599
www.dukeskauai.com
Hours: L 11:00 AM-11:30 PM
           D 5:00 PM-10:00 PM
Cards: AE DC DIS MC V
Dress: Resort Casual
Style: Amer/Sea $$

Menu Sampler:

Breakfast:
N/A

Lunch:
Barefoot Bar—Mac Nut and Dungeness Crab Wonton $6.95, Duke's Nachos $7.95, Beachside Burger $6.45, Stir-Fry Chicken Cashew $8.95, Pizzas $7.95, Fresh Fish Tacos $8.95, Large Caesar Salad with grilled chicken or mahi $9.95

Dinner:
Each selection includes our salad bar serving Duke's tossed Caesar Salad, freshly baked muffins, and sourdough bread. Fresh island fish prepared several ways such as baked in a garlic, lemon and sweet basil glaze, or marinated in shoyu and ginger, grilled and served with papaya lime relish, or roasted firecracker which is with tomato, chili, cumin aioli and served with black beans, Maui onion, and avocado relish, grilled with pineapple salsa, or Parmesan and Herb Crusted sautéed and topped with lemon and capers—all at $Market Price. Prime Rib $i7.95/$24.95, Seafood Coconut Curry-Thai Style-with fish, shrimp, and scallops served on white rice $17.95, Shrimp and Steak $19.95

Impressions:

Duke's Kauai is located down the beach from the Kauai Marriott Resort. This large open-air restaurant is built around an indoor tropical garden that would fit right in on a Hollywood sound stage. Even the tabletops are made from native woods and have been labeled with their island names. The terraced dining room and spacious Barefoot Bar offer patrons a front seat on Nawiliwili Bay. Dinner is the main event at Duke's with the mid-range steak and seafood menu served in generous portions. A light menu is available throughout the day for those looking for a late lunch or just coming in off the beach.

Kauai Dining

Lihue

Gaylord's at Kilohana
Kilohana Plantation
3-2087 Kaumualii Hwy
Lihue. HI 96766
808-245-9593
www.gaylordskauai.com
Hours: B (with tour only)
        L 11:00 AM-3:00 PM Mo-Sa
        D from 5:00 PM
        Su Bru 9:30 AM-3:00 PM
Cards: AE MC V
Dress: Resort Casual
Style: Amer/Cont $$$

Menu Sampler:

Breakfast:
Buffet with Tour Reservations Only-Call for Details
Sunday Brunch: Penne Alla Puttanesca served with garlic toast $14.95, Flame Broiled Hawaiian Au'ku with sunrise papaya and sweet basil butter sauce, steamed jasmine rice, garden vegetables $14.95, Chef Andy's Okinawan Sweet Potato hash with local purple sweet potato and chicken breast, two poached eggs and Maltaise sauce $13.95, Yellowfin Caesar Salad with parmesan chips $14.95
Lunch:
Entrées: Jambalaya Fettucine with garlic toast $9.95, Kilohana Meat Loaf with home-made mashed potatoes, corn relish, brown butter sauce $8.95
Dinner:
Appetizers: Won Ton Wrapped Prawns with wasabi plum sauce $9.95
Entrées: Crusted Sea Bass with macadamia nut crust, banana pineapple chutney, Okinawan purple potato, lilikoi carrots, garden vegetable $25.95, Farm Raised Venison on mascarpone & white truffle polenta, wild mushrooms in raspberry mango chutney sauce, baby lilikoi carrots, garden vegetables $31.95

Impressions:

Gaylord's is as much an event as a dining venue. The owners started out with a grand old plantation house and built on that foundation by adding dining, a luau, shops and carriage rides. This doesn't mean that their culinary efforts have been diluted. Quite the contrary! The courtyard dining area serves an extensive menu with an identity of its own. We see their approach as a global mélange. One could readily describe this experience as genteel, romantic, or gracious.

West Side

Grinds Café
4469 Waialo Road
Eleele, HI 96705
808-335-6027
www.grindscafe.net
Hours: BLD 5:30 AM – 9:00 PM
Cards: JCB MC V
Dress: Casual
Style: Amer/Ec/Isl $

Menu Sampler:

Breakfast:
Served All Day. Skillets are served with rice or potatoes. Portuguese Skillet with grilled Portuguese sausage, onions and green peppers with white cheeses $7.50, Farmers Skillet with homemade sausage grilled with green peppers and onions smothered with homemade country gravy $7.50, Omelets are served with rice or potatoes. Chili & Cheddar Cheese Omelet $6.95, Smoked Turkey, Mushrooms, and Monterey Jack Cheese Omelet $6.50, Mahi Mahi Breakfast of grilled mahi, choice of rice or potatoes, and two eggs any style $7.50, Loco Moco $6.50

Lunch:
Sandwiches: All come with condiments and choice of bread. Italian Sandwich $6.50, Super Veggie Sandwich $6.00, Cajun Ono Sandwich $7.00, Crispy Chicken Sandwich with grilled mushrooms, jack cheese and Dijon mustard $7.00, Grinds Burger (1/2 #) $6.25, Swiss Mushroom Burger $6.75

Salads: Chicken Walnut Salad topped with hot sliced chicken slices $9.75, Italian Salad with red onion ranch dressing $9.00, Organic Caesar $8.75

Pizza: 12", 15" and 18", Wheat or white crust with a wide variety of toppings. The Sicilian $16.50/$19.50/$26, The Veggie $16.00/$19.00/$24.00, Cajun Chicken 416.00/$19.50/$25.00, Canadian Bacon Pineapple $15.00/$18.00/$22

Dinner:
Mahi Mahi lightly breaded, grilled and served with homemade tartar sauce, rice and choice of mac salad or cole slaw $8.25, Cajun Ono with sides $7.50

Pastas: Cajun Chicken Linguine with green peppers, onions, celery and carrots and Cajun Sauce $14.50, Veggie and Pesto Linguine $12.50, add Ono $3.50

Impressions:

Grinds is an affordable little place along the highway on the way to the Waimea Canyon. This local eatery does it all--all day long. Their breads and pastries are baked in house adding a nice touch to the big portions and extensive menu.

Lihue

Hamura Saimin Stand   Authors' Favorite
2956 Kress Street
Lihue, HI 96766
808-245-3271
Web: None
Hours: L/D 10:00 AM-11:00 PM Mo-Th
       L/D 10:00 AM-1:00 AM Fr-Sa
       L/D 10:00 AM-9:30 PM Su
Cards: None
Dress: Casual
Style: Island $

Menu Sampler:

Breakfast/Lunch/Dinner:
Saimin-noodle soup with a garnish of green onions, fish cake and chopped ham
in small $3.75, medium $4.00, large $4.25, and ex-large $4.50, or Wun Tun
Mein-saimin with pork and shrimp filled dumplings $5.25, Special Saimin
$5.50, Extra Large Special Saimin $6.50, All extras $1.25, Shrimp Saimin with
two pieces deep fried tempura shrimp $5.50, BBQ Sticks-grilled chicken or beef
skewers dipped in a teriyaki sauce $1.25 each, Lilikoi Chiffon Pie $2.00 per
piece or a whole pie $10.75, Udon $4.25, Pretzels $2.00, Fried Noodles $4.00,
Soda $.80, Bottled Water $1.25, Malasadas-MoWeFrSa-2/$1.00

Impressions:

Time travel to Old Hawaii is today's reality at Hamura's Saimin Stand. Take
your place at the diminutive counter lined with tiny stools zigzagging across the
front of this plantation-style building and let the ladies dish you up some of the
best Asian style noodle soup you've ever tasted. Don't be shy about sitting next
to another customer and talking story. Everyone is friendly and will offer advice
about the hot mustard and other condiments. Order a BBQ Stick with your bowl
of saimin, and you're on your way to living local. One word of caution though,
only Hawaiians and teenage boys have enough stamina to finish an extra large
serving at Hamura's, so think about ordering something smaller.

Over by the side door you'll see the shave ice and halo halo stand with tropical
flavored syrups and extras like li hing mui and azuki beans. But then the lilikoi
chiffon pie is excellent. At $2.00 a slice, why not give it a try? This cultural icon
can get very crowded around lunchtime, so plan accordingly.

Kauai Dining

North Shore

Hanalei Dolphin Restaurant
5-5016 Kuhio Hwy (Hwy 56)
Hanalei, HI 96714
808-826-6113
www.hanaleidolphin.com
Hours: L 11:00 AM-3:30 PM, Light Menu 3:30 PM-5:30 PM
        D 5:30 PM-10:30 PM
Cards: MC V
Dress: Casual
Style: Sea/Stk $$$

Menu Sampler:

Breakfast:
N/A
Lunch:
Fin Burger charbroiled or Cajun with lettuce, tomato and onion $9, Calamari Sandwich-deep-fried, lettuce, tomato, and onion $8, Fish & Chips in beer batter with fries $11, Main Dish Salads $6-$9, Seafood Chowder-cup/$3, bowl/$6
Dinner:
Appetizers: Artichoke Crowns stuffed with garlic, butter, bread crumbs and cheese $8, Ceviche of raw fish marinated in lemon juice with tomatoes, celery, chili, Chinese parsley and green olives $6, Sashimi Plate $Mkt
Entrées: All entrees are served with a family style salad with our own dressing, penne pasta, steak fries, rice, or marinated veggie kabob, and hot homemade bread. Baked potato a la carte $2.50 with condiments. Fresh Scallops baked in wine, smothered in mozzarella $27, Dolphin Shrimp baked in butter and wine with our special seasonings topped with sour cream $27, Hawaiian Chicken-breast marinated in soy sauce and ginger $20/child's plate $16, 8 oz. Filet Mignon $28, Fish 'n Chips $20, Australian Lobster 20-24 oz. $Mkt
Desserts: Dolphin Ice Cream Pie $7, New York Cheesecake $5, Sundae $5

Impressions:

For us this open-air restaurant catches the magic of the Hanalei Valley. It sits alongside the river and at night the tiny lights in the palms and plants reflect upon the water. This traditional steak and seafood house has been around for a long time. The menu avoids trendy contrivances and comes at you straight on. There is a fish market in the back of the building, so you can be sure that the catch of the day is truly fresh. Plan ahead as reservations are not accepted.

Lihue

Hanama'ulu Restaurant
3-4291 Kuhio Hwy (Hwy 56)
Lihue, HI 96715
808-245-2511
Web: None
Hours: L 9:00 AM-1:00 PM Tu-Fr
         D 4:30 PM-Close Tu-Su
         D Buf 5:30 PM-8:30 PM Su
Cards: MC V
Dress: Casual
Style: Chi/Japan $$

Menu Sampler:

Breakfast:
N/A
Lunch:
Deluxe Chinese Plate Lunch-soup, fried chicken, fried shrimp, chop suey, crisp won ton, sweet and sour spare ribs, char siu or kau yuk, served with rice and tea $9.00, Japanese Special Plate Lunch includes miso soup, rice and tea and includes choice of one-calamari steak, sukiyaki with tofu, tonkatsu, teriyaki fish, teriyaki beef, teriyaki chicken, fish tempura, donburi $7.50, Won Ton Soup $8
Dinner:
Pupus: Crispy Won Ton $6.00, Spring Rolls $8.50, Potstickers $8.50
Entrées: Pork and Vegetables with tomato $9.00, Beef and Broccoli with mushrooms $9.00, Crisp Fried Ginger Chicken $7.50, Shrimp Canton $10.50, Shrimp Tempura with traditional dipping sauce $12.00, Tofu Tempura $6.50
Complete Dinners: Family Style 9 Course Chef's Deluxe Chinese or Chef's Special Japanese Dinners $19.95 per person, Hanama'ulu Special Platter $17.50
Oriental Buffet: Sunday Nights 5:30-8:30 PM $20.95
Dessert: Azuki Tempura $4.00, Green Tea Ice Cream $3.00

Impressions:

The proper name of this establishment used to be the Hanama'ulu Restaurant, Tea House, Sushi Bar, and Robatayaki. Try putting that in a phone book! This rambling 80-year old restaurant can be found on the Lihue bypass across from the 7-11. Add a touch of the exotic to your evening by making a reservation in one of their traditional Japanese tatami rooms. This is a sleeper. Don't judge it by curb appeal. Those looking for a local dining experience will be happy they came. Park in the lot just north of the building and enter through the gates.

West Side

Hanapepe Café   **Authors' Favorite**
3830 Hanapepe Road
Hanapepe, HI 96716
808-335-5011
Web: None
Hours: L 11:00 AM-3:00 PM Mo-Th
        L 11:00 AM-2:00 PM Fr
        D 6:00 PM-9:00 PM Fr
Cards: MC V
Dress: Casual
Style: Org $$

Menu Sampler:

Breakfast:
N/A
Lunch:
Beverages: Fresh Pressed Apple Juice 1.50, Herbal iced tea 1.75, Tropical fruit smoothie 3.50, Fresh squeezed orange juice 3.00, Sparkling mineral water 1.50
Soups & Salads: Served with fresh baked focaccia bread. House Caesar 7.00, Grilled Vegetable Salad with grilled tofu 9.00, Small side salads 3.50
Specialties: Crepe du Jour 10.00, Frittata with smoked mozzarella, sautéed mushrooms and veggies 8.50, Pasta du Jour $Daily Price, Lasagna-layers of seasonal vegetables between mozzarella and parmesan cheese 9.75, Chili & Rice with a choice of cheddar cheese 8.50, other announced specials available.
Sandwiches: served on your choice of focaccia, multi-grain, sourdough, or Ezekiel bread with Kauai's own Taro Chips. Hanapepe Healthnut Sandwich-hummus, Dijon, grilled onion, lettuce, tomato, cucumber, zucchini, yellow squash, red bell pepper 7.00, Garden Burger with Dijon, lettuce and tomato 6.00
Dinner:
Entrees: Eggplant Modugno-roasted eggplant rolls with an herbed cheese filling, an organic mesclun salad and tomato sauce, Seared Ahi Steak with Greek Skordalia Sauce, saffron potatoes, tomato tartlet 24.00.

Impressions:

This health-oriented restaurant really works. The menu intrigues, the service is caring, and the food delicious. Flavors are achieved through use of fresh herbs and spices rather than by adding extra salt or fat. Portions are substantial, but try to save room for their homemade desserts. Hanapepe is turning into a bit of an art colony making this a perfect fit.

Kauai Dining

East Coast

Hong Kong Café
Wailua Shopping Center
4-361 Kuhio Highway
Kapa'a, HI 96746
808-822-3288
Web: None
Hours: L/D 11:00 AM – 9:00 PM Mo-Fr
          L/D 2:00 PM – 9:00 PM SaSu
Cards: MC V
Dress: Casual
Style: Chi $

Menu Sampler:

Breakfast:
N/A
Lunch/Dinner:
Plate Lunches: Include two-scoop rice, one scoop mac salad, and chilled sweet & sour cabbage. Deep Fried Stuffed Eggplant $6.50, Char Siu $6.50, Duck with Ginger Chicken $6.50, Lup Cheong with Sweet and Sour Rib $5.95
Super Bentos: Crispy Chicken, Sweet & Sour Ribs, Kau Gee, Fried Shrimp, Vegetable Gon Lo Mein, Rice $6.95, Beef Broccoli, Lemon Shoyu Chicken, Kau Gee, Fried Shrimp, Vegetable Gon Lo Mein, Rice $7.50
Appetizers: Deep Fried Crab & Cheese Won Ton (6 pcs) $4.75, Deep Fried Won Ton (12 pcs) $2.50, Deep Fried Kau Gee (6 pcs) 4.50, S & S Sauce $.50
Soups: Won Ton Soup $6.50, Hot & Sour Soup (vegetarian) $6.95, Large Saimin $4.25, Crispy Chicken Saimin $5.95, Egg Drop Soup $6.25
Entrees: Sizzling Happy Family $10.95, Shrimp with Cashew Nuts $8.50, Kung Pao Chicken $7.25, Pork with Bitter Melon & Black Bean $7.25, Szechuan Broccoli $6.95, Roast Pork Choy Sum (Ham Ha) $7.50, Kung Pao Tofu $7.25
Specials: Sizzling Salmon Filet with black bean sauce $12.95, Sizzling Mahi with fresh dill and zucchini $13.50, Fresh Lemon Grass Snapper Wrap $12.95
Impressions:

This cozy little place features Chinese food cooked by chefs from China. Will wonders ever cease! The owner is a local realtor who divides his time between selling property and helping recent immigrants achieve their dreams of owning their own restaurants. The menu is varied and authentic, but the big hit is the specials board. Local products like fresh fish, Kauai shrimp, and homegrown herbs make their way to the kitchen daily. Things have gone a bit upscale lately.

Kauai Dining

North Shore

Java Kai Hanalei
Hanalei Center
Hanalei, HI 96714
808-826-6717
www.tastethefun.com
Hours:　6:30 AM-6:00 PM
Cards:　MC V
Dress:　Casual
Style:　Cof/Spec $

Menu Sampler:

Breakfast:
Collection of pastries, traditional offerings, and great Belgian waffles! Try the Kauai Waffle with papaya, banana, macadamia nuts and whipped cream on a fresh hot Belgian waffle for $7.95. Other treats are the Surfer's Sandwich with egg, bacon slices and cheese on an English Muffin $6.50, Bali Hai Burrito with eggs, potatoes, onions, tomatoes, cilantro, chili and cheese wrapped in a tortilla with papaya salsa and sour cream $8.95, Granola with milk or soy $5.95, Lattes, Smoothies, Chai, Juices, and Lemonade
Baked Items: Aloha Bars of toasted coconut, macadamia nuts and chocolate chips on a shortbread cookie crust; bagels, smoothies, specialty flavored coffee drinks, lemon bars, homemade muffins, apple pie, chocolate chip macadamia nut & oatmeal raisin cookies, shortbread with lemon topping.
Lunch/Dinner:
N/A

Impressions:

The first thing that strikes newcomers to Java Kai is the aroma of freshly brewed coffee. That's a great start, but these folks do a good job with their menu items as well. Customers order breakfast sandwiches and baked goodies at the counter for delivery to their table. Then it's time to while away a misty Hanalei morning. Nothing happens fast at this end of the road so take it easy and get into the vibe.

Lihue

JJ's Broiler
Anchor Cove Shopping Plaza
3416 Rice Street
Lihue, HI 96766
808-246-4422
Web: None
Hours: L 11:00 AM-5:00 PM
        D 5:00 PM-10:00 PM
Cards: DC DIS JCB MC V
Dress: Casual
Style: Amer/Pac Rim $$$

Menu Sampler:

Breakfast:
N/A
Lunch:
Hawaiian Ocean Chowder $6.75, French Onion Soup $6.75, Fish & Chips with seasoned fries and malt vinegar $11.95, Asian Grilled Chicken Salad with crisp vegetables and rice noodles served with hoisin dressing and a grilled chicken breast $10.95, Philly Steak Sandwich with rice or fries and pickle $9.95, Sautéed Mushroom Cheeseburger w/rice or fries and pickle $9.75, Fish 'n Chips $11.95
Dinner:
Appetizers, Salads & Soups: Onion Soup with glazed cheese and onion $6.25, Clam Bucket, 2 lbs. in white wine, garlic and herbs $19.95, Peking Chicken Taco of tender strips of chicken, shiitake mushrooms & vegetables wrapped in Peking pancakes with garlic oyster sauce $9.95, JJ's House Escargot $9.95
Entrées: All entrees include table salad bar & choice of steamed or house rice: Roasted Macadamia Lamb Rack with juniper garlic sauce $23.95, Prime Rib of Beef with au jus and horseradish $27.95, Coconut Shrimp with curried coconut crumbs, mango sauce and chutney $19.95, Beef Medallions with Lobster Sauce in a shiitake cream sauce $29.95, Hoisin Salmon Skewers on a warm soba salad with vegetables $23.95, Herbed Seafood Linguini with fresh basil, garlic $23.95

Impressions:

You'll find JJ's Broiler near the Marriott overlooking the beach on Nawiliwili Bay. Casual meals are served downstairs either inside or out on the lanai with the second floor open for dinner. Portions are quite generous, so sharing is an option. After work a lively crowd gathers in the lounge to enjoy their favorite adult beverages and relive the day's events.

South Shore

Joe's On The Green
2545 Kiahuna Plantation Drive
Poipu, HI 96756
808-742-9696
Web: None
Hours: B 7:00 AM-11:30 AM
        L 11:30 AM-2:30 PM
        D 5:30 PM-8:30 PM WeTh
Cards: MC V
Dress: Casual
Style: Amer $

Menu Sampler:

Breakfast:
Breakfast Specials include choice of hash browns or rice. Michael's Eggs Benedict $9.50, Create your own 3-egg omelet $8.50, J.B.'s Breakfast Burrito-a flour tortilla, beans, scrambled eggs, salsa, cheese, olives, and sour cream $8.25, French Toast $6.95, Banana Macadamia Nut Pancakes $7.75, Miso Soup $2.75, Anahola Granola $4.00, Half Papaya with yogurt or cottage cheese $3.75

Lunch:
"Personalized" House Salad served with a focaccia breadstick $7.25, New England Style Seafood Chowder-cup $3.25, with a half turkey or tuna sandwich $7.25, with a small house salad $6.95, or a bowl of chowder $5.50. Sandwiches are served with French fries, island coleslaw, potato-mac salad, or steamed rice. Joe's Mama Burger $7.95, Chicken Avocado with jack cheese-grilled $8.75. Lunch Specials are Fish and Chips w/cole slaw & fries $8.95, Linguini with Chicken-Artichoke Sausage & vegetables $8.50, Chicken Cutlet served with sautéed veggie's, rice and gravy $7.75, Loco Moco-1/3# hamburger $6.50

Desserts: Lilikoi Dream Ice Cream Pie $4.95, Kauai Ice Cream Pie $4.95

Dinner:
Wednesday & Thursday from 5:30-8:30 PM with live Hawaiian music

Impressions:

This popular dining spot is located in the golf course clubhouse at the beautiful Kiahuna Plantation. Going by the informal moniker of Joe's On The Green this establishment offers an affordable upscale alternative for residents and visitors alike. If you've watched birds trying to mooch a meal at the island restaurants, wait until you see the native island chickens try to outsmart the waitresses at Joe's. Hey, they live on Kauai too!

West Side

Kalaheo Coffee Co & Café
22-2436 Kaumualii Hwy (Hwy 50)
Kalaheo, HI 96741
808-332-5858
www.kalaheo.com
Hours: B/L 6:00 AM-3:00 PM Mo-Fr
        B/L 6:30 AM-3:00 PM Sa
        B/L 6:30 AM-2:00 PM Su
Cards: MC V
Dress: Casual
Style: Cof/Spec $
        Ent Card

Menu Sampler:

Breakfast/Lunch:
Gourmet coffees, wonderful pastries and baked goods such as pie, caramel rolls, fruit scones, croissants, muffins and cinnamon buns are produced daily on the premises. Belgian Waffles $5.95, Pancakes $5.25, Eggs with Portuguese sausage, ham or bacon, toast $5.75, Bonzo Burrito Tortilla Wrap with sautéed ham, peppers, mushrooms, onions and olives scrambled with two eggs, wrapped in a burrito with cheddar and Monterey jack $7.95. **Sandwiches** include soup, potato or green salad; Hot Pastrami Kalaheo Style on fresh baked bread $7.95, Grilled Herb Chicken Salad $9.75, Soup & Salad Combo $6.75, Grilled Country Style Reuben $7.95, Grilled Garden Burger $8.45, Tuna Salad Melt $7.75
Coffees: Café Au Lait, Red Eye, Black Eye, Espresso Americano, Hot Chocolate, Spiced Chai, Iced Coffee, Cappucino, Latte, Mocha
Dinner: N/A

Impressions:

Kalaheo Coffee Co & Café is a serve-yourself-at-the-counter kind of place with a menu that has taken on a life of its own. Although you couldn't really call this a restaurant there are a few tables available for limited seating. The reasonably priced breakfast and lunch offerings are surprisingly interesting and varied for this style of meal service. The staff is friendly and the surroundings are pleasant, but it's the baked goods that keep bringing us back. Consider including this stop when road tripping to Barking Sands Beach or Waimea Canyon.

West Side

Kalaheo Steak House
4444 Papalina Road
Kalaheo, HI 96741
808-332-9780
Web: None
Hours: 6:00 PM-10:00 PM
Cards: AE DIS MC V
Dress: Resort Casual
Style: Stk $$$

Menu Sampler:

Breakfast/Lunch:
N/A
Dinner:
Appetizers: Steamer Clams by the pound $5.95, Mussels- ½ # steamed in Tabasco, butter, garlic, green onions and lemon juice $5.95, Teriyaki Steak Stix of sirloin and strip loin skewered and marinated in teriyaki and barbecued $4.75, Mushrooms sautéed w/butter, garlic, red wine topped with Parmesan cheese & parsley $6.25, Artichokes steamed in an herb marinade $6.75 (seasonal)
Entrées: All dinners include House or Caesar salad and rolls with baked potato or white rice sliced bread and butter. Top Sirloin-12 oz.-$18.75, with a teriyaki marinade $18.95, Prime Rib slow roasted for 8 hours with au jus gravy and blended horseradish sauce- 12 oz cut $24.95/$28.95, Teriyaki Chicken Breast $16.95, Cornish Game Hen, marinated, oven roasted, flame broiled, topped with parmesan and chopped parsley $16.95, Baby Back Pork Ribs roasted then flame broiled with sauce $18.95, Kalaheo Shrimp sautéed in butter, lemon and fresh garlic, topped with parmesan and parsley and served on white rice $19.95, Alaskan King Crab Legs-1# $28.95, Broiled Fresh Island Fish $Market Price, Combos are offered $20.95/$24.95
Side Orders: Portuguese Bean Soup $4.95, Scalloped Potatoes $2.95
Desserts: Rum Cake & Ice Cream $3.95, Melinda's Cheesecake $4.95

Impressions:

Kalaheo Steak House has the friendly atmosphere you expect to find in a small town dining spot. However, as soon as you open the menu you're back on Main Street. This restaurant offers a metropolitan steak and seafood menu without the usual big-city prices. To find this little gem, drive a few miles south from Poipu Beach to Kalaheo and take a left at the stoplight on Papalina Road. Then go one block, look on your left, and you've found it. A small parking lot is off to the side of the building and there is plenty of street-side parking.

South Shore

Keoki's Paradise
Poipu Shopping Village
2360 Kiahuna Plantation Drive
Poipu, HI 96756
808-742-7535
www.keokisparadise.com
Hours: L 11:00 AM-11:00 PM
        D 5:00 PM-10:00 PM
Cards: AE DC DIS JCB MC V
Dress: Resort Casual
Style: Stk/Sea/Island $$

Menu Sampler:

Breakfast:
 N/A
Lunch:
Plate Lunch has "two scoop" rice. Choices are Koloa Pork Ribs $9.95, Grilled Island Fresh Fish $12.95, Hawaiian Fish and Chips $9.95, Stir-Fry Chicken Cashew $9.95, Veggie and Cashew Stir Fry $8.95, Bamboo Special $Mkt **Sandwiches**: Keoki's Fish Sandwich $11.95, Keoki's Paradise Burger $7.95, Cheeseburger $8.50, Tuna & Cheddar $6.95, Grilled Roast Beef & Cheddar $7.95. Cobb Salad $9.95, Grilled Chicken Caesar Salad $10.95. Nachos $6.95
Dinner:
Pupus: Thai Shrimp Sticks-grilled and served with a tangy guava cocktail sauce $9.95, Panko Crusted Scallops with Wasabi Butter Sauce $9.95.
Fish: Prepared five different ways-baked or sautéed with sauces $21.95-$25.95
Entrées: All entrées are served with Keoki's Caesar Salad & a basket of freshly baked bread. Coconut Crusted Chicken with coconut & mango sauce $15.95, Prime Rib $21.95/$29.95, Koloa Pork Ribs Asian Style glazed with plum sauce $18.95, Pesto Shrimp Macadamia over rice pilaf $17.95

Impressions:

Those in search of bamboo, torches, umbrella drinks, and live Hawaiian music will love Keoki's Paradise. This is Hawaii as it never really was except in the minds of Hollywood set designers. Who cares? It's fun anyway. After the drinks are served you'll be presented with a menu featuring old-time favorites prepared with island twists. Portions are generous and come at reasonable prices. This combination attracts a lively crowd and makes for a fun time. Keoki's is a large place with lots of parking. The long hours make this a great late night stop.

North Shore

Kilauea Bakery & Pau Hana Pizza   Authors' Favorite
Kong Lung Center
Kilauea. HI 96754
808-828-2020
Web: None
Hours: Pizza 11:00 AM-9:00 PM
         Bakery 6:30 AM-9:00 PM
Cards: MC V
Dress: Casual
Style: Spec $

Menu Sampler:

Breakfast:
Coffee made by the cup in the bakery with scones, and sweet cinnamon buns. Breakfast pastries and Danishes use mango, cheese, lilikoi, coconut, and Key Lime flavors. Full service gourmet coffee and espresso bar available.
Lunch/Dinner:
Tuscan Style Pizza as traditional or as gourmet as you like it. Sizes are small 8", medium 12", and large 16" ranging in price from $7.65-$29.25. Fresh vegetables, seafood, meats, specially prepared vegetables, and assorted cheeses make any combination possible. Specialty Pizzas are small $11.75, medium $19.50, and large $27.25 and are wonderful gourmet combinations such as Pomodoro-fresh tomatoes, Kilauea goat cheese, house marinated artichokes, black olives and mozzarella cheese, or the Billie Holliday of smoked ono, Swiss chard, roasted onions, gorgonzola rosemary sauce, and mozzarella cheese.
Soup & Salad: Kailani Farms organic lettuce blend, carrots, purple cabbage, tomato, organic sunflower sprouts and crispy croutons $6.25, Soup du Jour

Impressions:

Take the turnoff from the main highway to the Kilauea National Marine and Wildlife Reserve and you will find yourself in the small north shore village of Kilauea. Then follow the road toward the Kilauea Lighthouse until you reach the Kong Lung Center. There in the garden courtyard resides the Kilauea Bakery & Pau Hana Pizza. This is a very popular place with the locals—they line up in the morning with their coffee cups in hand. You'll know why when your eyes start to shine after the first cup! The pastries are an excellent accompaniment to their specialty coffees and teas. Lunch and dinner patrons find the pizza to be hearty, authentic, and delicious. There are a few indoor and outdoor tables for dining convenience. This is a great stop while you're out exploring the North Shore.

Kauai Dining

East Coast

Kountry Style Kitchen
1485 Kuhio Highway
Kapa'a, HI 96746
808-822-3511
Web: None
Hours: BL 6:00 AM-2:00 PM
Cards: MC V
Dress: Casual
Style: Amer $

Menu Sampler:

Breakfast:
Ham & Cheese Omelette with hash browns or rice, toast & jelly or cornbread $7.25, 8 oz. Steak & Eggs with hashed browns or rice, toast & jelly or cornbread $11.75, Omelette Bar $5.00 plus $1.45 for meats, $1.25 for cheese, $1.00 for veggies, 3 Banana or Strawberry Pancakes $5.25, French Toast $5.00, Fresh Chilled Papaya $1.75, Loco Moco $5.50, Eggs Benedict with hash browns or rice $8.75, Garden Benedict with mushrooms, spinach, tomatoes, and olives served with hash browns or rice $8.25, Keiki Specials $3.25-$3.50

Lunch:
All burgers are served with Krispy Fries. Burger Bar $4.75 plus mushrooms & bacon $1.50 each, plus cheese & veggies $1.00 each, BLT or Patty Melt served with French fries or potato salad $7.25, Grilled Mahi Mahi with vegetables, rice or fries, tartar sauce and hot corn bread $9.25, Kountry Fried Chicken (3 pcs) with rice or fries, vegetables, and hot corn bread $7.25, Chef Salad $7.25

Dinner:
N/A

Impressions:

The Kountry Style Kitchen Restaurant is a classic small town coffee shop set in the middle of the Pacific. This version is located in a roadside storefront on the north end of Kapaa. Inside customers crowd the booths and tables as waitresses weave thru with coffee pots held high. A handwritten specials board completes the scene. The atmosphere is comfortable and welcoming helped along by the homey menu offerings. Quality ingredients are used and the solid fare delivers as intended. As this is the mid-point of Kauai's single road highway system those doing the tour will find it to be a convenient stop.

East Coast

La Playita Azul
4-831 Kuhio Hwy
Kapa'a, HI 96746
808-821-2323
Web: None
Hours: L 11:30 AM-2:00 PM Tu-Fr
         D 5:30 PM-9:00 PM
Cards: AE MC V
Dress: Casual
Style: Mex $$

Menu Sampler:

Breakfast:
N/A
Lunch/Dinner:
Entrees: Tacos Dorados-two crispy tacos with shredded beef or chicken, salsa fresca, guacamole, rice and beans $9.95, Chicken Mole Enchilada-two chicken enchiladas served with homemade mole sauce, rice and beans $10.95, Quesadilla filled with cheese and chicken or beef, served with rice, beans, guacamole and sour cream $10.95, Chimichanga with an herb flour tortilla stuffed with chicken or beef, deep fried and served with rice and beans $10.95, Burrito Con Pollo with shredded chicken, rice and beans, and fresh tomatillo or tomato sauce $10.95, Taco de Pescado-two soft shell tacos made with sautéed fresh fish, served with salsa fresca, rice and beans $12.95, Chile Rellenos-traditional chile poblano stuffed with Monterey jack cheese, served with a fresh ranchero sauce, rice, beans, and tortillas $13.95, Fajitas of grilled chopped steak or chicken and fresh mixed vegetables, served with rice, beans, tortillas $15.95, Camarones Al Mojo De Ajo (garlic shrimp) served with rice, beans, tortillas $17.95, Camarones Ala Diabla-large shrimp sautéed in a chipotle sauce with rice, beans and tortillas $17.95, Seafood Burrito-an herb flour tortilla stuffed with jumbo scallop, shrimp, fresh fish, sautéed mixed vegetables, rice and beans and a fresh sour cream-jalapeño sauce $19.95, Seafood Fajita $24.95

Impressions:

La Playita Azul is another of the storefront eateries so common in Hawaii. It isn't very large, but the kitchen does a great job serving an extensive menu of authentic Mexican specialties. This isn't just a taco house. Besides the quick lunch items we all enjoy, they offer upscale entrees made with steak, chicken, and fresh seafood. Dining is very casual with seating both inside and out.

East Coast

Lemon Grass Grill   Authors' Favorite
4-885 Kuhio Highway
Kapa'a, HI 96746
808-821-2888
Web: None
Hours: D 5:00 PM-9:30 PM
Cards: AE DC DIS JCB MC V
Dress: Resort Casual
Style: Japan/Pac Rim $$$

Menu Sampler:

Breakfast/Lunch:
N/A
Dinner:
Starters: Tempura Fried Ahi of nori wrap with seasoned rice, ahi, deep fried, masago and wasabi aioli $8.75, Kalua Won Ton with ginger sweet potato, lomi tomato, poi vinaigrette, pineapple relish and our Kalua won ton $7.25
Salads: Moloa'a Shrimp and Papaya Salad with local greens, papaya, sprouts, pine nuts served with the spicy mango vinaigrette dressing $7.25
Specialties: Jumbo Scallop Sauté with jade sauce, fried long rice, shiitake relish, garlic mashed potatoes and balsamic syrup $19.00, Broiled Herb Lamb Loin with ratatouille, garlic mashed potatoes, pineapple relish and lamb au jus $20.95, Hoisin BBQ Chicken Breast with slaw and won ton pi, black bean relish, pineapple relish, and papaya relish $15.25, Huli Huli Chicken $15.25
Sushi Bar: Nigiri Sushi $3.50-$7.50, Cut Rolls- 9-1-1 of spicy tuna roll topped with avocado, katsuo bushi $9.50, Rainbow $9.50, Hand Rolls-California $4.00, Spicy Tuna $5.00, Eel $5.00, Sushi Combos-Waipoli Combo with miso soup, maguro, sake, Hamachi, ebi, Tamago, and California Roll $14.50, Viva Las Vegas Roll of tempura shrimp, crab, ahi, cucumber, deep fried and served with a sweet, spicy sauce $12.50, Spider Roll of soft shell crab and cucumber $11.50

Impressions:

Our first impression upon entering Lemon Grass was, "Wow! What a beautiful wood building!" Inside, you go up a staircase to the main dining room or stay downstairs for lanai dining. The sushi bar is unique with floating boats that were originally intended to convey fresh creations to diners. Unfortunately the turns proved too tight so the boat parade ended, but the sushi just keeps coming. After sampling the sushi experience, don't miss out on the Pacific Rim inspired menu. You won't find some of these innovative preparations elsewhere.

Kauai Dining

Lihue

Lihue Barbecue Inn
2982 Kress Street
Lihue, HI 96766
808-245-2921
Web: None
Hours: B 7:00 AM-10:30 AM XSu
          L 10:30 AM-1:30 PM XSu
          D 5:00 PM-8:30 PM XSu
Cards: MC V
Dress: Casual
Style: Amer/Filip/Japan/Haw $$

Menu Sampler:

Breakfast:
Shortstack Special of two pancakes, one egg and choice of either bacon or Portuguese sausage $5.95, Three Egg Omelet with chicken, onions, tomatoes, green peppers, spinach and cheese $8.95, Oriental Breakfast of miso, fish teriyaki, egg with green onions, tsukemono, and steamed rice $7.95

Lunch:
All entrees and sandwiches include soup or fresh fruit, dessert and choice of coffee or tea. Grilled or Sautéed Fish of the Day with fruit salsa $12.95, Teriyaki Steak Sandwich $5.95, Hamburger $4.50, Katsu Donburi $8.95, Ahi Sandwich with choice of slaw, fries, or tossed greens $9.95

Dinner:
Appetizers: Tri-Sampler of fire-grilled chili rubbed prawns served with a BBQ Hollandaise sauce, furikake deep fried squid with honey-curry dipping sauce, and seared teriyaki top sirloin $16.95, Winter Crab Cakes w/curry sauce $14.95
Entrées: Baby Back Ribs $19.95, Baked Stuffed Mahi Mahi w/snow crab, veggies & cheese, Dijon & ginger aioli $18.95, Mac Nut Crusted Chicken Breast w/papaya/pineapple marmalade $18.95, Rack of Lamb w/chutney $23.95
Desserts: The greatest homemade cream pies in flavors such as peanut butter, chocolate, lemon, banana, cherry, etc. $1.25 per slice!!

Impressions:

Years ago soldiers used to line up in the street to enjoy the Lihue Barbecue Inn's home-style food and atmosphere. Not that much has changed as a solid group of loyal customers keeps the friendly staff busy serving an extensive list of island favorites. Selections and prices cross a wide spectrum. The café decor includes booths and tables, but as an added twist there is a separate lounge area.

East Coast

Mema Thai Chinese Cuisine
Wailua Shopping Plaza
4-369 Kuhio Hwy (Hwy 56)
Kapa'a, HI 96746
808-823-0899
www.hanaleihaven.com
Hours: L 11:00 AM-2:00 PM XSaSu
          D 5:00 PM-9:00 PM
Cards: AE DC DIS MC V
Dress: Casual
Style: Chi/Thai $$

Menu Sampler:

Breakfast:
N/A

Lunch/Dinner:
Appetizers: Shrimp Rolls of rice paper stuffed with long rice, onion, black mushrooms, water chestnuts and shrimp served with lettuce, mint leaves and cucumber $7.95, Sa-teh—coconut milk, peanut butter, kaffir lime leaves, seasoning, cucumber sauce on the side, choices are tofu or vegetable $7.95, Chicken on the Stick $8.95, Fish battered and deep fried $10.95, Shrimp $10.95
Soups: Thai Ginger Coconut Soup with kaffir lime leaves $7.95-$14.95, Long Rice Soup $7.95-$10.95, Spicy Lemongrass Soup with Shrimp $10.95
Salad: Fresh Island Papaya Salad $6.95, Calamari Salad w/lemongrass $10.95
Noodles and Rice: Pad Thai of stir fried Thai rice noodles with eggs, chives, and bean sprouts topped with peanuts and lemon on the side-chicken or pork $9.95, shrimp $11.95, seafood $17.95, Broccoli Noodles with Pork $9.95
Entrées: Fried Garlic Pork with garlic & black pepper served on a bed of chopped cabbage with sweet & sour sauce $9.95, Pad Ped $8.95-17.95, Lemon Chicken $8.95, House Curry with kaffir lime leaves, fresh ground lemon grass, peas and coconut milk- chicken, pork, or beef $9.95, Mema's Beef Curry $9.95

Impressions:

Mema Thai is located across the highway from Restaurant Kintaro at the south edge of Kapa'a. As you walk up to the door, the first things you'll notice are the rosewood furnishings and art objects that give this restaurant its distinctive and exotic atmosphere. From there the enticing aromas take off and give a hint to the fabulous flavors to be experienced herein. Thai food will never be referred to as boring. This is affordable dining with panache.

North Shore

Neide's Salsa & Samba
Hanalei Center
5-5161 Kuhio Highway
Hanalei, HI 96714
808-826-1851
Web: None
Hours: L 11:30 AM-2:30 PM
       D 5:00 PM-Closing
Cards: MC V
Dress: Casual
Style: Braz/Mex $

Menu Sampler:

Breakfast:
N/A
Lunch/Dinner:
Mexican Dishes:
Macho Burrito with refried beans, cheese and onions, choice of shredded beef, chicken, pork or veggies, topped with ranchera sauce, melted cheese, sour cream and black olives $8.95, Huevos Ranchera of two eggs sunny side up on a crisp, flat corn tortilla with refried beans, ranchera sauce, sour cream and black olives, served with Spanish rice and flour tortilla $8.95, Nachos w/black olives $4.50
Brazilian Dishes: Panqueca of a crepe with pumpkin stuffing and fresh vegetables, smothered in Neide's own special sauce with melted cheese and fresh vegetables & cheese served with Brazilian rice $9.95, Ensopado of chicken and fresh vegetables baked with a special Brazilian sauce, served with Brazilian rice and black beans $10.95, Bife Acebolado-a tender, juicy beef steak smothered in fresh Maui onions, served w/Brazilian rice and black beans $15.95
Child's Plate: Choice of a taco, enchilada, or quesadilla served with Spanish rice and beans $6.50

Impressions:

Neide's Salsa & Samba is located in the back of the Hanalei Center and shares a courtyard dining area with Bamboo Bamboo. If it rains take a seat in the indoor dining room set with wooden tables and chairs. Since opening in '98 Neide's has developed a loyal following of locals and visitors who enjoy their large servings of Mexican and Brazilian dishes. For those new to Brazilian cuisine, it is long on meat courses and comes in sizeable portions. All of the entrées served here are mildly seasoned, as in the Brazilian tradition.

Kauai Dining

East Coast

Norberto's El Café
4-1373 Kuhio Hwy (Hwy 56)
Kapa'a, HI 96746
808-822-3362
Web: None
Hours: D 5:00 PM-9:00 PM XSu
Cards: AE DIS MC V
Dress: Casual
Style: Mex $$

Menu Sampler:

Breakfast:/Lunch:
N/A
Dinner:
All dinners are served with soup, Spanish rice, refried beans, corn chips, and plenty of hot Mexican salsa. Burrito Ranchero of shredded or ground beef $15.45, Beef Tostada-Enchilada Combination made with a crispy corn tortilla with seasoned beef, refried beans, cheddar cheese, lettuce, Spanish enchilada sauce, and tomatoes served with one jack and cheddar cheese enchilada $15.45, Rellenos Tampico-a select green chile stuffed with natural Monterey Jack cheese, dipped in whipped egg and sautéed to a golden brown, with Spanish sauce and cheese and a tasty cheese enchilada $17.95, Mex-Mix Plate with a chicken chimichanga, a chicken taquito, and a cheese enchilada with guacamole $17.95. A la carte items range from a $4.75 Taco, $8.95 for a Nachos Supreme, $9.45 for a Burrito Outrageous, to $14.45 for a Rellenos Plate for adults.
Dessert: Hula Pie $3.50, Rum Cake 3.50, Ice Cream $2.50

Impressions:

Norberto's has been around Kapa'a Town so long we sometimes wonder which came first, the restaurant or the building. The menu is traditional zesty Mexican with some notable twists. First, in order to meet heart-healthy standards, no lard or animal fat is used. Then, as a concession to the local clientele, many dishes may be requested vegetarian. In fact, one of their house favorites is an enchilada stuffed with eggplant rather than meat. For a Hawaiian touch the restaurant also features homegrown taro leaf enchiladas. Fish specials are offered when they're available. The cantina in the back serves Margarita's by the glass or pitcher as well as domestic and imported beer.

East Coast

Ono Family Restaurant   **Authors' Favorite**
1292 Kuhio Hwy (Hwy 56)
Kapa'a, HI 96746
808-822-1710
Web: None
Hours: B 7:00 AM-1:00 PM
       L 11:00 AM-2:00 PM
Cards: AE DC JCB MC V
Dress: Casual
Style: Amer/Island $

Menu Sampler:

Breakfast:
Eggs Hash--corned beef hash with two poached eggs, toast, side of hollandaise and a slice of papaya $7.75, Eggs Canterbury-poached eggs, ham, turkey, jack cheese, tomato, hollandaise sauce and mushrooms on an English muffin with a slice of papaya $8.95. Three-Egg Omelets include a wide choice of fillings, & a choice of hash browns, rice, fried rice or toast $6.25-$8.75, Tropical Stack with bananas, macadamia nuts, coconut, and whipped cream $6.50
Lunch:
Farmer's Sandwich of turkey, ham, jack cheese, lettuce, tomato and mayonnaise on Branola bread with French fries and soup $8.25, Chicken Breast Plate served with rice or fries and choice of teriyaki or BBQ sauce and soup or salad $8.95, Saimin-Chinese noodle soup topped with wonbok, carrots, green onions, & a half hard-boiled egg-small $4.25, large $6.25, Burgers served with fries or salad $6.20-$8.20, Oriental Chicken Salad with a stir-fried chicken breast $8.25
Dessert: Coconut or Macadamia Nut Custard Homemade Pie $3.95/slice.
Dinner:
N/A

Impressions:

This plantation-style restaurant is a great breakfast or lunch choice. The lengthy menu features two pages of egg dishes alone! Ingredients such as homemade chorizo, lup cheong, and kim chee reflect the multi-cultural population of the island. Although steamed rice or potatoes accompany most offerings, the fried rice is a real hit. This local and visitor favorite is full of aloha style hospitality and is a "must try" for the adventurous traveler.

West Side

Pacific Pizza & Deli
9852 Kaumualii Highway
Waimea. HI 96796
808-338-1020
Web: None
Hours: L/D 11:00 AM-9:00 PM
Cards: DIS MC V
Dress: Casual
Style: Amer/Spec $

Menu Sampler:

Breakfast:
N/A
Lunch/Dinner:
Pizzas & Calzones:
Pacific Pepperoni Pizza-S $7.25, M $11.95, L $16.25/Pepperoni Calzone $4.75
Surfa Deluxe with pesto sauce, Canadian bacon, shrimp, faux crab, pineapple-S $8.95, M $14.95, L $19.95/Surfa Deluxe Calzone $5.50
Lomi Lomi with cheeses, fresh tomatoes, diced salmon, diced onions & green onions-S $8.95, M $14.95, L $19.95/Lomi Lomi Calzone $5.50
Hapa Haole with pesto sauce, cheeses, sun-dried tomatoes, mushrooms, zucchini, olives, Canadian bacon, and pineapple-S $8.95, M $14.95, L $19.95/Hapa Haole Calzone $5.50
Portuguese with our own Portuguese sausage, onions, and olives & more - S $8.50, M $13.95, L $18.95/Portuguese Calzone $5.00
Cold Wraps with turkey, chicken, roast beef, pastrami, ham or veggies $5.25-seafood $6.25 in a tomato-basil tortilla with our own special dressing
Deli Sandwiches with choice of meat and bread with fresh toppings $5.25

Impressions:

Located in a large plantation style building alongside Wrangler's Steakhouse you'll find the Pacific Pizza & Deli. High ceilings, wood floors, and antiques are a proper setting for the quality pizza and calzones coming out of the kitchen. The yeasty crust is puffy on the edges while thin and crispy in the center, even with all the toppings. Sometimes it is difficult to obtain good Italian sausage in the islands, but theirs' has that tantalizing taste of fennel. A small pizza will feed two people generously making this a very affordable stop for lunch or dinner.

East Coast

Panda Garden
4-831 Kuhio Hwy
Kapa'a, HI 96746
808-822-0092
Web: None
Hours: L 10:30 AM-2:00 PM X We
         D 4:00 PM-9:30 PM
Cards: AE DIS JCB MC V
Dress: Casual
Style: Chi $$

Menu Sampler:

Breakfast:
N/A
Lunch/Dinner:
Appetizer: Spring Roll $4.95, Shrimp and Bacon Roll $5.95, Squid with Pepper
Salt $10.95, Steam Dumpling $5.95, Roasted Pork $5.50, Fried Kau Gee $4.50
Soup: Bird's Nest Soup $10.95, Minced Chicken Cream Corn Soup $6.50
Seafood: Kung Pao Shrimp $9.95, Sweet and Sour Shrimp with Pineapple
$9.95, Squid with Garlic-Ginger Sauce $9.95, Lobster Tail w/Black Bean Sauce
$19.95, Scallop w/Chinese Peas $10.95, Sesame Shrimp $9.95
Chicken: Curry Chicken $7.95, Dry Fry Chicken $8.95, Hong Kong Crispy
Chicken $7.50, Sesame Sauce Chicken $8.95, Lemon Chicken $7.95
Beef: Mongolian Beef $8.50, Beef with Black Mushroom $8.95, Beef with
Oyster Sauce $7.95, Green Onion Beef $8.50, Beef with Green Pepper $8.50
Pork: Shredded Pork with Garlic-Ginger Sauce $8.50, Steam Pork Hash $8.50
Other Entrees: Duck with Oyster Sauce $8.95, Mu Shu Pork $9.50, Seafood
Pineapple Fried Rice $9.95, Seafood Hong Kong Noodle $11.95
House Specialties: Walnut Shrimp $14.95, Szechuan Triple Crown w/Gulf
shrimp, tender beef & pork -hot & spicy $13.95, Orange Flavored Beef $12.95
Lunch Specials: Mo-Fr 10.30 AM-2:00 PM-served w/soup, fried won ton, &
rice-Cashew Nut Chicken $6.95, Mongolian Beef $7.95, Beef w/Broccoli $6.95
Family Dinners: $13.95/$16.95 per person (two person minimum-one entrée
choice per person) includes Spring Roll, Soup, Entrees and Rice

Impressions:

Panda Garden might be located in a storefront, but it is definitely a restaurant.
Besides their solid Hong Kong and Szechuan menu, they offer full bar service
and an attractive facility. Find them in the Kauai Village Shopping Center.

South Shore

Pattaya Asian Café
Poipu Shopping Village
Poipu, HI 96756
808-742-8818
Web: None
Hours: L 11:30 AM-2:30 PM Mo-Sa
       D 5:00 PM-9:30 PM
Cards: MC V
Dress: Casual
Style: Thai $$

Menu Sampler:

Breakfast:
N/A

Lunch/Dinner:
Appetizers: Fish Cakes (5) Chopped string beans mixed with fish and deep fried, served with cucumber peanut sauce $8.95, Summer Rolls (2) wrapped in rice paper with sliced cabbage, carrots, bean sprouts, basil, chopped peanuts and rice noodles with house dipping sauce-vegetable $7.95/shrimp $8.95

Soups & Salad: Spicy Lemon Grass Soup-seafood $15.95, Fresh Island Papaya Salad $6.95, Shrimp Salad w/onion, cucumber, mint leaves, lettuce $10.95

Noodles and Rice: Chicken Pad Thai $9.95, Bell Pepper with Noodles and Tofu $9.95, Broccoli Noodles with pork $9.95, Pineapple Fried Rice with Shrimp $11.95, Spicy Fried Rice with vegetables $9.95, Sticky Rice $2.25

Ala Carte: Pad Ped-Eggplant, red chili, coconut milk and fresh basil with fish $11.95, Evil Jungle Prince-seafood combo- with sweet basil, sautéed in coconut milk, with red chili on a bed of cabbage $16.95, Pineapple with Curry Sauce and hot red chili, coconut milk on a bed of long thin rice noodles-shrimp $11.95, Broccoli with Chicken, Pork or Beef and Oyster Sauce $9.95

Curries: Pork Green Curry with lemon grass, kaffir lime leaves, eggplant and fresh basil $9.95, House Curry-Famous Siam Style Panang-fresh ground lemon grass, peas, kaffir lime leaves, and coconut milk with seafood $16.95

Impressions:

Thai food aficionados visiting Poipu Beach can satisfy their culinary cravings with a stop at the Poipu Shopping Village. There in the courtyard you'll find a cozy little Thai restaurant serving all the traditional favorites. Full bar service is offered for those so inclined. This place represents good value considering that you can spend $6.00 for a hot dog on this part of the island.

East Coast

Pedro's Texas Barbeque
Waialua Shopping Plaza
4-361 Kuhio Highway
Kapa'a, HI 96746
808-822-5722
Web: None
Hours: D   4:00 PM-9:00 PM Mo
          LD 11:00 AM-9:00 PM Tu-Fr
          LD 12:00 PM-9:00 SaSu
Cards: MC V
Dress: Casual
Style: Amer $

Menu Sampler:

Breakfast:
N/A
Lunch/Dinner:
From The Pit: Served with homemade beans and choice of one side, white bread and barbeque sauce. Classic Texas Brisket $9.95, Pulled Pork Plate $8.95, Barbeque Chicken Plate $7.95, Pecan Smoked Turkey Plate $9.95, Cowboy Ribeye $14.95, Rib and Chicken Combo $14.95, Louisiana Hot Links $7.95
Sandwiches: Served on bun w/potato-mac salad/slaw. Pulled Pork $7.95, Texas Beef Brisket $7.95, Big "D" Steak & Cheese $9.95, Smoked Turkey $8.95
BBQ Emergency Kit: Ribs, Barbeque Chicken, Brisket, Sausage, Slaw, Corn, Potato Mac Salad, Beans-family style-each person $13.95, 2 person minimum.
Sides: Homemade Potato Mac Salad $1.80, Cole Slaw $1.80, Barbeque Beans $2.50, Steamed Corn on the Cob $.95, Corn Bread Plain $1.50, Jalapeño and Cheese Corn Bread $1.75, Dill Pickles $.75, Steamed Rice $1.50
Specials: Jambalaya with shrimp, chicken, and Cajun Ham $6.95/$13.95, Cajun Fried Shrimp Basket with fries or slaw $11.95, Cajun Smoked Shrimp $12.95, Southern Fried Chicken Basket-3 pieces with slaw or fries $8.95, Chicken Fried Steak with country gravy, mashed potato, and one side $8.95
Desserts: Daily Selection

Impressions:

Texas barbeque on Kauai? Yep! Pedro's is a small storefront establishment in a strip mall behind Mema Thai. Southern specialties complement their delicious smoked meats creating an experience not often found in the islands. Everything is available packed as carryout for a beach picnic or the condo crowd.

Kauai Dining

South Shore

Pizzetta
5408 Koloa Road
Koloa, HI 96756
808-742-8881
Web: None
Hours: L 11:00 AM-3:00 PM
        Happy Hour 3:00 PM-6:00 PM
        D 4:00 PM-9:00 PM
Cards: MC V
Dress: Casual
Style: Amer/Ital $$

Menu Sampler:

Breakfast:
N/A
Lunch:
Sandwiches & Pasta: Veneto of blackened chicken, Cajun dressing, mozzarella cheese, lettuce & tomato w/pasta salad $6.95, Homemade Meatball-oven baked w/marinara, roasted garlic cream sauce & mozzarella, open-faced w/pasta salad $6.95, Pasta Lunch Special-penne w/choice of sauce, house salad & bread $7.95
Pizza: Thin Crust or Regular. Medium $14.95-$17.95, Large $18.95-$22.95, additional toppings-Medium $1.75, Large $2.25 each, Slices only $2.95-$3.70
Happy Hour: 3:00 PM-6:00 PM
Dinner:
Antipasti, Salads & Sides: Hot Crab & Artichoke Dip with Crostini $9.95, Garlic Bread Sticks with marinara sauce $5.95, Caesar Salad $4.95/$7.95
Entrees: Fettuccini Quattro Formaggio $10.95, Chicken Marsala w/penne Marsala or garlic mashed potatoes $16.95, Eggplant Parmesan w/pasta or garlic mashed potatoes $13.95, Lasagne $13.95, Fettucini Lucia w/olive oil, fresh garlic, parmesan cheese, feta cheese, chicken breast, sun dried tomatoes $15.95
Pizza: Handmade herb crust thin or regular, medium or large $13.95-$22.95, Pizza By The Slice $2.95-$3.70 served 11:00 AM-6:00 PM

Impressions:

After several days of fine dining you might crave a casual, affordable meal. That is where Pizzetta comes in. Here you will find pizza parlor favorites served in a convivial family atmosphere. This happening spot is not just for visitors though, as local folks like to gather here for happy hour and revelry late into the evening. Delivery is free anywhere on the south shore.

South Shore

Plantation Gardens
Kiahuna Plantation Resort
2253 Poipu Road
Poipu, HI 96756
808-742-2216
www.pgrestaurant.com

Hours:	5:30 PM-10:00PM
Cards:	AE DC MC V
Dress:	Resort Casual
Style:	Pac-Rim/Med $$$

Menu Sampler:

Breakfast/Lunch:
N/A

Dinner:
Pupus: Crab and Rock Shrimp Stuffed Shiitake Mushrooms imu baked with macadamia nut aioli $10.95, Island Shrimp & Fresh Fish Wontons with mango guava chili sauce $9.95, Mixed Sashimi Platter with wasabi shoyu sauce $12.95
Salads: Caesar Salad with macadamia nut garden pesto croutons and pecorino cheese $7.95, Spinach & Arugula Salad w/balsamic basil vinaigrette $8.95
Entrées: House Smoked Pork Tenderloin, sugar cane skewered, grilled tamarind hoisin plum sauce, caramelized Maui pineapple $19.95, Jumbo Scallops Stir Fry-smoked bacon wrapped scallops, kiawe grilled, Koloa asparagus, Asian vegetable stir fry and soba noodles $17.95, Seafood Lau Lau-fresh catch, seafood, and local spinach wrapped in ti leaves $22.95, Double Cut Lamb Chops, fresh herb & Dijon crust, pan seared, ginger mint apple sauce and Madeira lamb jus $24.95, Hawaiian Hot Pot-Sugar Cane Skewered Shrimp & Scallops, fresh local fish, simmered in gingered coconut fish broth, Asian noodles and peanut oil $22.95, Filet Mignon, gorgonzola smoked bacon polenta and shiitake Maui onion demi-glaze $25.95

Impressions:

This historic plantation home with its high ceilings, cherry floors, koa trim and hand-painted murals was once home to the manager of the Kiahuna Plantation. Today it's a luxurious open-air dining venue serving award-winning Pacific Rim cuisine with occasional Mediterranean spins. Whether enjoying pupus in the lounge or dining on the veranda, a gracious island experience awaits.

South Shore

Poipu Bay Grill & Bar
2250 Ainako
Koloa, HI 96756
808-742-1515
Web: None
Hours: B 7:00 AM-10:30 AM Mo-Fr
         B 7:00 AM-11:00 AM Sa
         L 10:30 AM-2:30 PM Mo-Fr
         L 11:00 AM-2:30 PM Sa
         BL 7:00 AM-2:30 PM Su
Cards: AE DC DIS JCB MC V
Dress: Casual
Style: Amer/Isl $$

Menu Sampler:

Breakfast:
Poipu Delight-trio of pancakes with blueberries, bananas and mango 8.75, Broke Da Mouth! – three-egg frittata w/Portuguese sausage, provolone cheese, tomatoes, green onion & fried rice 9.75, Dungeness Crab Hash, two poached eggs w/dilled hollandaise sauce 13.75, Keoneloa Breakfast Sandwich of homemade sweet bread roll, stuffed w/bacon or ham, two eggs your way & melted cheese 9.75, Two Eggs, Meat, rice or potatoes, toast, preserves 9.75

Lunch:
Blackened Hawaiian Chicken Roll with salsa, guacamole, sour cream 9.50, Pacific Rim Chicken Salad in won ton cup with Chinese mustard vinaigrette 14.50, Portuguese Bean Soup 6.50, Poipu Bay's Fish & Chips with garlic fries and coleslaw 13.50, Crab Melt-Poipu Bay's Signature Dish-crab served on an English muffin with two cheeses 14.50, Stir Fry of the Day, rice 13.50

Desserts: Poipu's Bay's Chocolate Thunder-vanilla ice cream, chocolate brownie chocolate chunks, warm chocolate and caramel sauce 7.00

Impressions:

Those who remember grabbing a cup of coffee and a sweet roll before teeing off will appreciate this place more than most. Clubhouse dining has come of age in this gracious room overlooking the Hyatt course. The menu offers a level of sophistication in line with the mega-facility. Preparations lean toward complex where traditional dishes involving exotic ingredients are tweaked with island techniques. The wait staff follows through providing attentive, friendly service. History buffs might enjoy the ancient heiau (temple) alongside the parking lot.

South Shore

Poipu Beach Broiler
1941 Poipu Road
Koloa, HI 96756
808-742-6433
www.pbbroiler.com
Hours: L 11:30 AM-3:00 PM
        D 5:00 PM-10:00 PM
        Happy Hour 2:00 PM-5:00 PM
Cards: AE DIS MC V
Dress: Resort Casual
Style: Isl/Pac-Rim $$

Menu Sampler:

Breakfast:
N/A
Lunch:
Appetizers: Baby Back Ribs w/bourbon-pineapple $10, Island Style Hot Wings $10, Vegetable Spring Rolls $8, Blue Point Oysters $10
Salads: Salad Bar $7, Caesar Salad with lemon anchovy vinaigrette $7
Main Courses: Fish & Chips w/fries & lemon remoulade sauce $9, Teriyaki Chicken Sandwich with caramelized pineapple $8, Fresh Ahi Tuna Sandwich $8
Dinner:
Appetizers: Lobster & Crab Ravioli $10, Sautéed Mushrooms $8
Entrées: Macadamia Mahi Mahi pan fried & served with jasmine rice and Kahana Royale beurre blanc $18, Blackened "Daily Fish" $23, Grilled Ahi or Ono $23, Southwestern Spiced Ahi $23, Baby Back Pork Ribs with Hawaiian salt baked potato, house made bourbon & pineapple bbq sauce $22, Grilled Pork Chop $19, Slow Roasted Prime Rib $23, Top Sirloin Steak $20
Desserts: Chocolate Mousse $6, Luau Dream Sorbet $5

Impressions:

This used to be The House Of Seafood. A few years ago new owners appeared and took the place down to the bare walls. Not only did the atmosphere improve but so did the menu. Chef Brant Hunt prepares exciting dishes with layers upon layers of flavor. His gift is taking something common and adding spins to come up with results that far exceed the sum of the parts.

West Side

Pomodoro Restaurant
Rainbow Plaza
2-2514 Kaumualii Hwy (Hwy 50)
Kalaheo, HI 96741
808-332-5945
Web: None
Hours: D 5:30 PM-9:30 PM XSu
Cards: MC V
Dress: Resort Casual
Style: Ital $$

Menu Sampler:

Breakfast/Lunch:
N/A

Dinner:
All dinners include our home baked foccacia.
Antipasti: Calamari Fritti $11.50, Mozzarella Marinara $7.50, Prosciutto & Melon (or seasonal fruit) $8.50
Insalate: Caesar $7.95, Mixed Greens with light balsamic vinaigrette $6.95
Zuppe: Minestrone alla Pomodoro $4.25
Pasta: Spaghetti with Bolognese or Marinara Sauce $12.95, with meatballs $13.95, Tortellini alla Panna $15.95, Manicotti filled with a blend of cheeses $14.95, Lasagne (House Special) with Italian sausage and choice beef $15.95, Linguini with white or red clam sauce $16.50, Fettuccine Alfredo $13.95
Specialties: All dishes are served with farfelle pasta with seasonal vegetables. Veal Pizzaiola with roasted peppers and onions in our special wine sauce $21.95, Chicken Saltimbocca $19.95, Eggplant Parmigiana $18.95, Scampi $21.95, Veal Scaloppini Al Marsala $21.95, Scampi in a fresh garlic, caper and wine sauce $21.95, Veal Piccata $21.95, Calamari Steak Parmigiana $18.95
Desserts: Assorted Italian desserts daily $6.50

Impressions:

This intimate bistro-style restaurant is located on the second floor of the Rainbow Plaza at the eastern edge of Kalaheo. After cocktails, dinner begins with prompt and professional servers delivering the authentic Italian cuisine for which this family-run establishment is known. Afterwards there is a wonderful dessert tray to tempt you. For this kind of quality combined with reasonable prices, a visit to Pomodoro is definitely worth the short drive from Poipu.

North Shore

Postcards Café
5-5075A Kuhio Hwy (Hwy 56)
Hanalei, HI 96714
808-826-1191
www.postcardscafe.com
Hours: D 6:00 PM-9:00 PM
Cards: AE MC V
Dress: Casual
Style: Sea/Veg $$

Menu Sampler:

Breakfast/Lunch:
N/A

Dinner:
Pupus: Island Taro Fritters-polenta crusted with pineapple chutney salsa $9.00, Thai Summer Rolls, fresh or seared with spicy peanut sauce $9.00, Salmon Rockets wrapped in lumpia with a sweet spicy chili sauce $10.00, Porcini Crusted Scallops sautéed with mushrooms & greens, cashew-date dressing $10.00, Butterfly Prawns broiled, served with pineapple-coconut-macadamia topping $10.00, Cajun Crusted Ahi with chipotle chili sauce $11.00
Salads: Poki Salad with cucumbers, celery, red onions, scallions, diced tofu and sesame tamari marinade $6.00, Caesar Salad with homemade croutons $8.00
Entrées: Seafood Sorrento-a pasta with medallions of fresh fish and shrimp sautéed with onions, mushrooms, tomatoes, bell peppers, Kalamata olives and capers in a garlic-sherry sauce $22.00, Taj Triangles are warm phyllo crescents filled with seasonal vegetables and spices with a delectable sauce and fresh tropical chutney $17.00, Thai Coconut Curry with fresh vegetables & tempeh sautéed with Thai spices over organic rice with pungent peanut sauce $17.00, Island Fish grilled or blackened, with rice, vegetables and a choice of sauces-honey ginger Dijon, macadamia nut butter, or peppered pineapple sage $Mkt

Impressions:

Look for the quaint plantation cottage home of Postcards mauka of the highway as you enter Hanalei. Indoor/outdoor dining is offered in this picturesque village setting. The vegetarian oriented menu features natural and organic ingredients, although fish and shellfish are offered. This little spot seems to attract its fair share of celebrities and loyal patrons, so call ahead as dinner reservations are necessary. Hours are subject to change seasonally.

East Coast

Restaurant Kintaro   Authors' Favorite
4370 Kuhio Hwy (Hwy 56)
Kapa'a, HI 96746
808-822-3341
Web: None
Hours: D 5:30 PM-9:30 PM XSu
Cards: AE DC DIS JCB MC V
Dress: Resort Casual
Style: Japan $$

Menu Sampler:

Breakfast/Lunch:
N/A
Dinner:
Sushi: Maki Sushi (cut rolls) and Temaki Sushi (hand rolls) Kilauea Roll-slightly smoked salmon, tuna (ahi), avocado, & Maui onions $9.00/half roll $5.50, Shrimp Tempura Roll with cucumber, radish sprouts & tobiko rolled in seasoned rice & seaweed $10.00-with unagi $12.95, Nigiri Plate $13.95
Appetizers: Lemon Buttered Mussels in shell (4 pcs) $3.95, Gyoza -fried dumpling (5 pcs) $5.50, Crispy Won Ton from owner's factory (8 pcs) $3.50
Dinners: Served with chilled buckwheat noodles and sauce, miso soup, rice, Japanese pickles and tea. Tempura Combination of local fish, shrimp, and a variety of fresh vegetables $13.95, Yakitori-chicken with onion, bell pepper, teriyaki sauce and salad $13.50, Various Nabemono $10.95-$14.95
Teppan Yaki: Chef is entertaining as he prepares the meal on a tableside grill. Dinners are served with miso soup or salad, shellfish, seafood, mushroom, and fresh island vegetables prepared teppan style. Oysters sautéed with olive oil $14.95, Filet Mignon $20.95, Hibachi Shrimp $17.95, Island Chicken Teriyaki $14.95, Steak Teriyaki $19.95, Fresh Island Fish with Scallops $Market Price
Nabe Mono: One pot chafing dish with seafood and vegetables $10.95, $14.95

Impressions:

Even though Restaurant Kintaro is much larger than it looks from the outside, you need to decide which style of Japanese dining you're interested in before making reservations. This rambling establishment offers a sushi bar, teppanyaki tables, teishoku, and tatami seating. If we had to choose one place on Kauai to experience Japanese cuisine this would be it. As one patron said, "Best sukiyaki I ever had, and I eat it a lot". Reservations are a must in this popular place.

South Shore

Roy's Poipu Bar & Grill
Poipu Shopping Village
2360 Kiahuna Plantation Drive
Poipu, HI 96756
808-742-5000
www.roysrestaurant.com
Hours: D 5:30 PM-9:30 PM
Cards: AE DC JCB MC V
Dress: Resort Casual
Style: Haw-Reg $$$

Menu Sampler:

Breakfast/Lunch:
N/A
Dinner:
Appetizers: Minted Chicken & Basil Spring Rolls w/sweet chili peanut vinaigrette $8.50, Shrimp & Asparagus Crepes w/chevre, pesto & rosemary demi-glace $1150, Seared Shrimp-on-a-stick w/spicy wasabi sauce $10.50
Salads: Granny Smith Apple & Gorgonzola Salad w/candied walnuts & a sesame miso vinaigrette $8.50, Greens w/sesame soy rice wine vinaigrette $6.50, Hau'ula Tomato Carpaccio Salad with mozzarella, capers 9.50
Entrées: Jade Pesto Steamed Hawaiian Whitefish w/a Chinese sizzling cilantro ginger peanut oil $29.50, Asian Seared Peking Duck Breast w/ a star anise mango basil sauce $28.50, Imu Roasted Pork Pot Roast w/ a pineapple ginger apple sauce $19.50, Yama Mama's Meatloaf with onion rings & mushroom pan sauce $8.50/ $17.50 (entrée), Hibachi Style Salmon with a citrus ponzu sauce $14.50/$29.50 (entrée), Garlic & Honey Mustard Short Ribs w/fresh poi & lomi tomatoes $25.50, Kiawe Grilled Tiger Shrimp $26.50, 20-25 Nightly Specials

Impressions:

Chef Roy Yamaguchi was one of the founders of the Hawaii Regional Cuisine movement begun in the late '80's to promote the use of fresh local produce, fish, and meats in island cooking. His style of culinary fusion launched Roy's into the global marketplace of fine dining. Every dish offered at this casual but upscale eatery uses herbs and spices from diverse cuisines for a real taste explosion! Look for the nightly specials, and don't miss the dessert tray. Roy's in Poipu is smaller than some of his other locations, so reservations are an absolute must.

North Shore

Sabella's at Princeville   Authors' Favorite
5300 Ka Haku Road
Pali Ke Kua
Princeville, HI 96722
808-826-6225
Web: None
Hours: D 6:00 PM-9:00 PM
Cards: AE MC V
Dress: Resort Casual
Style: Isl/Ital $$$

Menu Sampler:

Breakfast/Lunch:
N/A
Dinner:
Appetizers: Pan Seared Scallops with lime aioli $14.00, Ahi Tartare, three oils and spicy crème fraiche $ Mkt, Baked Brie with white peaches and honey drizzles $12.00, Bacon Wrapped Shrimp with cucumber salad & mesquite vinaigrette $11.00, New England Clam Chowder $4.00/$6.00
Salads: Shrimp & Artichoke Salad with sunrise papaya & light vinaigrette 9, Grilled Peach & Dungeness Crab Salad, egg crumbles, bacon bits & greens 11, Kauai Goat Cheese Tomato Salad w/Maui onion, balsamic vinaigrette dressing $12.00, Mermaid Salad of fresh island seafood served over mixed greens $13
Main Courses: Crab & Bacon Stuffed Ono with sweet brandy reduction $25.00, Coriander Seared Salmon, orchetta pasta & greens $25.00, Apple Brandy Lobster-apples, bacon, brandy & chef's seasonings 40, Herb Crusted Rack of Lamb with honey cognac reduction $27.00, Chicken Saltimbocca Prosciutto with marsala sauce $23.00, Lasagna Angela $19.00, Eggplant Parmesan-dipped in egg, breaded, topped with fresh tomato sauce and parmesan cheese $19.00
Dessert: Tropical Sicilian Cannoli $8.95, Lopaka's Ice Cream Bananas sautéed in butter, brown sugar and a splash of rum with sorbet $14.00

Impressions:

North Shore visitors have a new dining option that really deserves consideration. A fourth generation restaurant family has taken over some space in the condos just before the Princeville Hotel and created Sabella's. We find their approach to be refreshing. Instead of muddling cuisines and risking fusion confusion, they offer two distinct styles kept true to their roots. This is all presented in classy surroundings perfect for an evening of leisurely dining.

South Shore

Sheraton Kauai Resort Restaurants
Sheraton Kauai Resort
2440 Hoonani Road
Poipu, HI 96756
808-742-4012
www.sheraton-kauai.com
Hours: See Below
Cards: AE DC JCB MC V
Dress: Resort Casual
Style: Ital/Stk/Sea/Japan $$$

Menu Sampler:

Galleria Dining Rooms
Shells: B-Traditional Breakfast Buffet $17.95, Extensive a la carte menu available.
D: Filet Mignon seared & roasted served w/cognac peppercorn sauce $30, Sautéed Opakapaka with a lemon caper sauce $28, Broiled Lobster Tail $36
Amore Ristorante: D-Lobster stuffed in half moon ravioli w/ricotta cheese in a light lobster lemon cream reduction $21, Sautéed Jumbo Shrimp in a garlic, white wine and butter with a touch of lemon on a bed of fettuccini $26
Naniwa: D-Wafu'u Steak of Black Angus Strip Loin Steak w/Sudachi ponzu radish sauce & sautéed vegetables $31/$37, Tekka Don $26/$32
The Point: 11 AM-Midnight. Portuguese Bean Soup $8.95, Coconut Shrimp w/Thai sweet and sour $16.95, Saimin $8.95, Vegetarian Spring Rolls $10.95, Cheese & Pepperoni Pizza $14.95, Triple Chip Nachos $10.95.
Entrees- 6-10 PM- Roasted Chicken w/garlic & rosemary glaze, mashed potatoes & veggies $19.95, NY Steak w/mashed potatoes $25.95
Oasis Bar & Grill: Grilled Angus Beef w/trimmings & fries $11.95, Fried Mahimahi Sandwich with fries $14.95, Turkey Club w/fries $11.95

Impressions:

The Sheraton Kauai Resort sits on one of the most beautiful stretches of beach on the entire island. Capitalizing on the hypnotic views, they have assembled a notable collection of dining rooms covering the waterfront from casual dining to international cuisine. Shells is the anchor serving the daily upmarket breakfast buffet before changing over to a steak and seafood format. When the time comes for drinks and pupus, don't miss sunset at The Point. Lunch service is available at the casual Oasis Bar & Grill while adventurous dinner patrons will find gourmet Italian in Amore Ristorante and outstanding Japanese in Naniwa.

East Coast

The Bull Shed

4-796 Kuhio Hwy (Hwy 56)
Kapa'a, HI 96746
808-822-3791
Web: None
Hours: D 5:30 PM-10 PM
Cards: AE DC DIS MC V
Dress: Casual
Style: Amer/Sea $$

Menu Sampler:

Breakfast/Lunch:
 N/A
Dinner: All dinners include steamed rice, bread & butter and a trip to the salad bar. Broiled Shrimp or Teriyaki Broiled Shrimp $15.95, Scallops Bull Shed-sea scallops sprinkled with parmesan cheese and baked in white wine sauce with sliced mushrooms $17.95, Prime Rib (house specialty) $23.95, Pork Baby Back Ribs $18.95, Garlic Tenderloin or Tenderloin Filet $20.95, Grilled Teriyaki Chicken $14.95, Garlic Chicken $14.95, Australian Lamb Rack-a full rack marinated in an herbal red wine recipe and broiled $26.95, Teriyaki Beef Kebobs broiled with crisp vegetables $9.95, Teriyaki Top Sirloin marinated in a sauce of brown sugar, pineapple juice and shoyu $15.95, Black Pepper Tenderloin, broiled, smothered in pepper sauce with onion, mushroom and beef au jus mix $20.95, Alaskan King Crab/Grilled Catch of the Day $Market Price Children's menu is available.
Desserts: homemade ice cream pies and cheesecakes $3.50

Impressions:

This oceanfront restaurant is Kauai's answer to supper club dining. With a salad bar, cocktail lounge, and prime rib in a starring role, this steak-and-seafooder strikes a note of comfort and familiarity. Although the interior décor is not a strong suit, the good food and friendly service continue to please. On warm evenings try to get a table by the windows for a cooling breeze. Finding the entrance can be an interesting experience. Look across the highway from the McDonald's at the Waipouli Town Center stoplight and follow the lane.

East Coast

The Eggbert's

Authors' Favorite

Coconut Marketplace
4-484 Kuhio Hwy
Kapa'a, HI 96746
808-822-3787
Web: None
Hours: B 7:00 AM-3:00 PM
         L 11:00 AM-3:00 PM
         D 5:00 PM-9:00 PM
Cards: MC V
Dress: Casual
Style: Amer $$

Menu Sampler:

Breakfast:
Eggs Benedict, ham $7.45/$9.75, with vegetables $7.95/$10.25, Eggbert's Unique French Toast (until 11 AM) $5.95, French Omelette-2 eggs $4.25, 3 eggs $5.65, with hash browns or toast, Denver Omelette with two eggs $7.65, with three eggs $8.75, Two Eggs, two pieces meat, rice or hash browns $6.25, Hotcakes $5.45, Fluffy Banana Hotcakes $5.95, Hotcakes $3.95/$4.95
Lunch:
BLT and chips $5.25, Fish Sandwich, grilled in butter, chips $6.50, British Burger, ¼ # with bacon, American cheese, Thousand Island dressing, mac salad $7.25, The Big "O"- an omelette sandwich with choice of ingredients $5.75
Dinner:
Soups: New England Clam Chowder $2.50/$3.50, Soup of the day $2.25/$2.75
Entrées: Meat Loaf, mashed potatoes, brown gravy, broccoli hollandaise, roll $8.95, Fresh Catch, choice of rice or baked potato, broccoli hollandaise $Mkt, Roast Pork, mashed potatoes, brown gravy, broccoli hollandaise, roll $9.25, NY Steak, rice or baked potato, broccoli hollandaise $14.50, Eggs Benedict, Burgers

Impressions:

The Eggbert's is an old Kauai institution. They were once located in Lihue before moving to the Coconut Marketplace. Breakfast is the big drawing card with service until 3 PM. When was the last time you were asked whether you wanted the eggs on your benedict prepared soft, medium or hard? Then select your choice of toppings before adding the best hollandaise on the island. The owners fill out the day with extensive lunch and dinner menus. This place specializes in mainland style comfort food done a cut above.

North Shore

The Hanalei Gourmet
The Old School House at Hanalei Center
5-5161 Kuhio Hwy
Hanalei, HI 96714
808-826-2524
www.hanaleigourmet.com
Hours: L 11:00 AM-9:30 PM
        D 5:30 PM-9:30 PM
Cards: AE DC DIS JCB MC V
Dress: Casual
Style: Amer/Isl $$

Menu Sampler:

Breakfast:
N/A
Lunch:
Primo Pupus: Asian Style Crab Cakes with pineapple aioli sauce 8.75, Artichoke Dip with French baguette and breadsticks 8.95, Artichoke Toast 4.95
Salads: Roasted Garlic Caesar 5.95/7.95, Mediterranean Salad with balsamic vinaigrette and focaccia bread 8.50, Hanalei Waldorf with fresh greens, caramelized walnuts, fresh sliced apples, gorgonzola crumbles, mango vinaigrette dressing 5.95/7.95, Chicken Salad Boat in a fresh papaya 8.95
Sandwiches: Oregon Bay Shrimp Sandwich with a New Orleans remoulade sauce 8.95, Dewey's Gorgonzola Burger with caramelized onions & fries 8.50
Dinner:
Pastas: Chicken Udon Stir Fry, mixed greens, focaccia bread 16.95, Shrimp Scampi, salad of mixed greens and focaccia bread 17.95, Pasta du Jour 13.95
Entrées: Beer Battered Fish & Chips with soy wasabi sauce, fries, Asian slaw $Mkt, Charbroiled Pork Chops with a spinach sauté 18.95, Mac Nut Fried Chicken with a guava lime sauce 17.95, Scallops Meuniere over croutes 21.95, Fresh Catch charbroiled, blackened or sautéed $Mkt, Charbroiled Rib Eye Steak seasoned with Hawaiian salt and black pepper, garlic mushroom sauté 25.95

Impressions:

Your first impression of this local favorite might be that you just walked into a belly-up-to-the-bar hangout. You did! But they have a lot more to offer than a shot-and-a-beer. Everyone from the wait staff to the kitchen help knows what they're doing. Better yet, there's a complexity to the food that belies the simple surroundings. Just about anyone can find something to like on this menu.

Kauai Dining

East Coast

The Hukilau Lanai
Kauai Coast Resort
520 Aleka Lp
Kapa'a, HI 96746
808-822-0600
Web: None
Hours: D from 5:00 PM XMo
Cards: AE DC DIS JCB MC V
Dress: Resort Casual
Style: Amer/Pac-Rim $$$

Menu Sampler:

Breakfast/Lunch:
N/A
Dinner:
Starters: Kona Lobster Curry Bisque 6.95, Sesame Chicken Salad 5.95, Sweet Potato Ravioli with Kilauea feta cheese and roasted Okinawan sweet potato in a lemon grass cream sauce 6.95, Kona Lobster & Goat Cheese Won Ton 9.95
Salads: Wally's Salad: romaine, cucumber, tomato, bacon, red onion & citrus tossed with a savory papaya seed dressing 2.95/4.95, Beach Boy Caesar Salad 3.95/5.95, Kauai Kunana Dairy Chevre Salad-greens tossed w/basil vinaigrette and garnished w/Kauai Kunana Dairy goat cheese & Kamuela tomato 4.94/6.95
Entrées: Oven Roasted Chicken with a shiitake mushroom veloute and basil red-skin mashed potatoes 15.95, Filet Mignon with Ulupalakua red wine sauce and tonight's special potato $Mkt, Sugar Cane Skewered Shrimp & Tropical Chicken Duet brushed with Dave's peanut barbeque sauce on orzo risotto 18.95
Desserts: Coconut Crème Caramel, baked Big island Vanilla Bean coconut custard in a pool of caramel sauce 5.95, Macadamia Nut Tart w/vanilla bean ice cream 6.95, Kauai Mocha Mousse Cake- a dense chocolate mousse made with Kauai coffee and coated in Ganache, served on a decadent brownie crust 6.95

Impressions:

This recent addition to the Kauai dining scene aims to please a variety of moods and tastes. On one hand the menu features old American favorites; while on the other diners can experience Pacific Rim cuisine. Meanwhile the kitchen takes a page out of the Hawaii Regional Cuisine book through the extensive use of local products. This all comes together in a comfortable dining room where relaxing over dinner is the norm. Make reservations at this popular spot.

Kauai Dining

North Shore

The Lighthouse Bistro
Kong Lung Center
2484 Keneke St
Kilauea, HI 96754
808-828-0480
Web: None
Hours: L 12:00 PM-2:00 PM XSu
          D 5:30 PM-9:00 PM
Cards: MC V
Dress: Resort Casual
Style: Euro/Pac-Rim $$

Menu Sampler:

Breakfast:
N/A
Lunch:
Fish Tacos of sautéed fresh fish, tomato, onion, cilantro and seasonings in a soft shell taco & salsa $9.95, Fish Burrito with black beans and cheese $11.95, Thai Chicken Wrap w/sweet Thai chili sauce $6.95, BLT $4.95, BBQ Chicken $6.95, Cheeseburger-cheddar cheese, lettuce, onion, tomato on sesame bun $5.95, Caesar Salad with fish $15.95, Garden Burger with lettuce, tomato $6.50
Dinner:
Appetizers: Coconut Shrimp w/sweet chili sauce & aioli $13.95, Fish Rockets - fish wrapped with furikake and lumpia served with a wasabi aioli $12.95
Soups & Salads: Caesar Salad $9.95, Kilauea Goat Cheese Salad $14.95
Pasta: All you can eat Pasta & Sauce Bar (4 pastas, 3 sauces) $13.95
Entrées: Fresh Fish grilled with a white wine lemon beurre blanc, tropical jasmine rice pilaf, and fresh vegetables $23.95, Filet Mignon Delmonico with a gorgonzola cheese burgundy sauce with mashed potatoes and vegetables $29.95, Pacific Saltimbocca-veal medallions with a prosciutto gorgonzola herb sauce, mashed potatoes, vegetables $27.95, Pineapple Pork Medallions $18.95

Impressions:

Dining options are limited on the North Shore of Kauai. This sparsely populated area can only support so much. When The Lighthouse Bistro opened in Kilauea, it was a welcome addition. Not only do they serve a respectable dinner menu, they also offer lunch for hungry travelers. Note that the price point has a wide range making this place affordable for various appetites and budgets.

Kauai Dining

South Shore

Tidepools   Authors' Favorite
Hyatt Regency Kauai Resort and Spa
1571 Poipu Road
Koloa, HI 96756
808-742-1234
www.kauai-hyatt.com
Hours: D 6:00 PM-10:00 PM
Cards: AE DC DIS JCB MC V
Dress: Resort Casual
Style: Contemporary Haw $$$

Menu Sampler:

Breakfast/Lunch:
N/A
Dinner:
Appetizer: Charred Hawaiian Ahi Sashimi with wasabi and sweet ginger dip 12.75, Kimo's Crab Cake with avocado salsa and passion fruit sauce 11.00, Award Winning Local Style Ahi Poke 10.50
Soup and Salads: Coconut Lobster Soup with Tahitian vanilla bean crème 7.50, East Kauai Onion Soup baked with four cheeses 7.00, Grilled Kauai Sweet Onions and Vine Ripened Tomatoes with Omao mizuna and arugula, Hanalei feta cheese and black pepper lychee vinaigrette 8.75, Big Island Baby Romaine Salad with Kauai Kunana feta cheese, rosemary and thyme vinaigrette 8.75
Entrées: Macadamia Nut Crusted Mahi with kahlua, lime, ginger butter sauce and served with jasmine rice 28.50, Seafood Mixed Grill-a selection of lobster, scallops, shrimp and island fish with stir-fry vegetables 34.00, Prime Rib with creamy horseradish 29.50, Roasted Sonoma Lamb Rack with eggplant and goat cheese risotto and oregano scented demi $41.00, Kauai Spiced Opah stuffed with lump crab meat, shiitake mushrooms and asparagus 29.00

Impressions:

Tidepools is the signature restaurant of the Hyatt Regency Kauai Resort and Spa. Dining here means sitting under a thatched roof surrounded by bamboo décor, torches, and koi fishponds while the ocean surf pounds in the distance. This is truly an Old Hawaii setting. The wait staff presents the freshest island ingredients fused in creative preparations. A must try is the Coconut Lobster Soup with Tahitian Vanilla Bean Crème. Don't pass up the dessert offerings! This is a personal favorite and would be a good choice for the splurge night. Reservations are strongly recommended.

Kauai Dining

Lihue

Tip Top Motel & Café
3173 Akahi Street
Lihue, HI 96766
808-245-2333
Web: None
Hours: B 6:30 AM-11:30 AM XMo
        L 11:00 AM-2:00 PM XMo
        D 5:30 PM-9:30 PM XMo
Cards: MC V
Dress: Casual
Style: Amer/Haw/Japan $

Menu Sampler:

Breakfast:
Ham & Cheese Omelet with rice or hash browns $6.50, Macadamia Nut
Pancakes $4.00/$4.50, Our Famous Oxtail Soup $7.35, Loco Moco $6.50, Sweet
Bread French Toast $4.00, French Toast $3.75, Fried Rice $3.50, Soft Fried
Noodles $5.50, Beef Stew $6.00Bento of chicken, corned beef hash, teri meat,
egg roll, goteburg sausage, potato salad, pickled vegetables, rice $6.25
Lunch:
All entrées and daily specials are served with vegetable, choice of rice, French
fries or mashed potatoes. Country Style Boneless Chicken $6.25, Pork Chops
$6.25, Baked Meat Loaf with gravy $6.00, Roast Pork $6.75, Hamburger $3.45
Dinner:
Sushi Combination of 7 different kinds of Nigiri Sushi and Maki Mono $19.95,
Chirashi Sushi-a fresh seafood combination artistically over vinegared rice
$16.95, Fresh Salmon Roll $5.00,Unagi Roll $5.50, Spicy Ahi Roll $5.50, Soft
Shell Crab Roll $6.95, Big California Roll $9.00, Assorted Sashimi $16.95
Entrees: Include soup & rice. Shrimp Tempura $12.95, Teriyaki Beef $10.95,
Chicken Katsu $9.50, Oyaku Donburi $8.95, Saimin Special $6.95

Impressions:

Are there motels in Hawaii? A few. Does this establishment cater mostly to
locals? Sure does. Is the food good? It is. The Tip Top Café offers local style
dining in spotless surroundings. A visit to the Tip Top is a cultural experience.
Local businessmen and groups of ladies as well as retirees and keiki gather in
the roomy booths to enjoy the local cuisine and discuss all that's happening in
Lihue. Oxtail Soup is a top choice in the café section of the restaurant during
breakfast and lunch. For a change of pace, there's sushi available at dinner.

Lihue

Tokyo Lobby
Pacific Ocean Plaza
3501 Rice Street
Lihue, HI 96766
808-245-8989
Web: None
Hours: L 11:00 AM-2:00 PM XSaSu
        D 4:30 PM-9:30 PM
Cards: AE JCB MC V
Dress: Resort Casual
Style: Japan $$

Menu Sampler:

Breakfast:
N/A
Lunch:
Sashimi and Sushi: Served w/soup. Nigiri asst $14.95, Inari Sushi $10.95
Donburi: Served with soup. Oyako Donburi of sliced chicken, onions, and eggs over rice with special sauce $6.50, Katsu Donburi of fried pork cutlet, onions, and eggs over rice with special sauce $7.50, Curry Chicken Donburi $6.95
Entrées: Served with soup, pickled vegetable, and rice. Shrimp and Vegetable Tempura $7.95, Yaki Sakana (Grilled Mackerel) $7.95, Katsu $7.95
Dinner:
Appetizer: Gyoza-seasoned ground pork wrapped in ravioli and pan-fried $4.50, Shu-Mai—shrimp dumplings $3.95, Edamame $2.95, Sashimi $9.50
Side Order: Miso Soup $1.50, Ochitashi—steamed spinach with light soy sauce $4.50, Oshinko (pickled vegetables) 4.50, Green Salad w/house dressing $4.50
Sashimi and Sushi: Served with soup. Sashimi with rice $13.95, Makimono Combination—nori rolled sushi $14.95, Sashimi Deluxe with rice $21.95
Entrées: Served with soup, pickled vegetable, salad and rice. Hibachi Lemon Herb Chicken $12.95, Beef Teriyaki $14.95, BBQ Salmon or Fish in season $13.95, Tokyo Love Boat-complete dinner for $22.50/person, min. of two

Impressions:

The menu at Tokyo Lobby can best be described as provincial Japanese. No, this isn't kaiseki dining, but it isn't local style either. The menu offers a wide variety of traditional Japanese dishes at very reasonable prices. Look for this restaurant on the first floor of the Pacific Ocean Plaza across from the Kauai Marriott. Ample parking is available in the shopping center lot.

North Shore

Tropical Taco
Halelea Building
5088 Kuhio Hwy (Hwy 56)
Hanalei, HI 96714
808-827-8226
www.tropicaltaco.com
Hours: 11:00 AM-5:00 PM XSu
Cards: None
Dress: Casual
Style: Mex $

Menu Sampler:

Breakfast:
N/A

Lunch/Dinner:
Tropical Taco-deep fried or just warm $6.95, Tropical Fish Taco-fish dipped in beer batter and fried golden brown or grilled $7.92, Regular Taco $4.50, Fat Jack—ten inches of flour tortilla with cheese, meat, beans, deep fried, topped with lettuce, salsa, cheese, and sour cream $7.92, Fresh Fish Burrito of catch of the day fried and topped with the works of beans, lettuce, salsa, cheese, and sour cream $6.96, Veggie Burrito-everything but the meat $5.76. Recently Roger added "taro tacos" made with taro grown behind his house.

Impressions:

Roger and Barbara Kennedy would like to welcome you to their new taco eatery in Hanalei. For a look at its predecessor ask to see the old green panel van where it all began. In days gone by that truck was Roger's taco shop. Local lore has it that during a hurricane back in the early '90's, Roger chained his taco truck to a palm tree in a desperate attempt to protect his investment and after donning a bicycle helmet rode out the storm inside! There is another version of the story that says he did it because his truck was safer than his house. We leave it up to you to decide which version you prefer.

Eventually Roger bowed to progress and relocated in the new Halelea Building. In order to remain true to the spirit of his original business, his artistically inclined friends designed a silhouette of the truck's side panel and mounted it on the kitchen wall of his new establishment. Through this "van window" orders are placed and delivered as they always have been. Fun people, nice restaurant, simple but tasty menu, very large portions, and a good time!

West Side

Waimea Brewing Co.
Waimea Plantation Cottages
9400 Kaumualii Hwy (Hwy 50)
Waimea, HI 96796
808-338-9733
www.wbcbrew.com
Hours: 11:00 AM-9:00 PM Su-Th
           11:00 AM-11:00 PM Fr-Sa
Cards: AE DC DIS MC V
Dress: Casual
Style: Amer/Island $$

Menu Sampler:

Breakfast:
N/A
Lunch/ Dinner:
Pupus: Ale Steamed Shrimp, ½ # served with sweet Thai chili sauce $12.95, Nui Nachos $10.95, Taro Leaf Goat Cheese Dip with grilled pita bread $9.50
Salads: Asian Chicken Salad w/citrus vinaigrette $10.95, Thai Beef $12.95
Sandwiches: All are served with brewpub fries & Java slaw. Kalua Pork Sandwich—pork roasted Hawaiian style topped with smoked provolone cheese on a Maui onion bun with lettuce, tomato and kosher pickle $10.95, Seared Poke Wrap with wasabi aioli and fresh veggies $11.95, Hawaiian Chicken Sandwich w/a slice of pineapple $9.75, Angus Beef Burger $8.95, Kalua Pork Wrap $9.50
Entrées: Kalua Pork on a abed of cabbage, kim chee, sticky rice $15.95, Jawaiian Chicken, Caribbean rice, black beans $15.95, Balsamic Glazed Strip Steak with wasabi mashed potatoes, veggies $19.95, Teriyaki Steak & Ale Shrimp, wasabi mashed potatoes, veggies $29.95, Kalbi Beef Short Ribs, sticky rice, veggies $18.95, Full Rack BBQ Ribs, potatoes or rice, veggies $24.95
Brews: Wai'ale'ale Ale, Pakala Porter, Captain Cook's Original India Pale Ale, and Na Pali Pale Ale, West Side Wheat, Leilani Light, Cane Fire Red

Impressions:

Want an unlikely scenario? How about finding a brewpub in an old plantation village at the end of the road in Waimea! The kitchen at Waimea Brewing Co. serves distinctive pupus and large servings of fun, tasty salads, sandwiches, and entrées in the pub or out on the veranda. After sightseeing on the sunny west side the surprisingly good on-site brewed beers offer a great way to cool off.

Kauai Dining

East Coast

Wasabi's On The Reef
4-1388 Kuhio Hwy
Kapa'a, HI 96746
808-822-2700
Web: None
Hours: L 11:00 AM-5:30 PM Mo-Fr
        D 5:30 PM-10:00 PM
Cards: MC V
Dress: Casual
Style: Japan $$

Menu Sampler:

Breakfast:
N/A
Lunch:
Teriyaki Chicken 8.95, Shrimp or Fish Tempura 9.95, Fresh Fish of the day
sautéed in teriyaki or sweet miso sauce or just seasoned 10.95, Vegetarian
Special of tofu and vegetable tempura with sautéed vegetables 7.95
Dinner:
Teriyaki Chicken 14.95, Shrimp or Fish Tempura 15.95, Fresh Fish of the day
sautéed in teriyaki or sweet miso sauce or just seasoned 16.95, Vegetarian
Special of tofu and vegetable tempura with sautéed vegetables 7.95
Lunch or Dinner Side Orders: Miso Soup 2.95, Edamame 2.95,
Lunch or Dinner Sushi House Specialty Rolls: Golden Roll of maguro,
smoked salmon, crab & avocado, served tempura style with an avocado-unagi
sauce 10.95, Lava Roll of smoked salmon with a mix of hamachi, crab, shrimp
& scallops with sake-mayo & avocado-unagi sauce 12.95, Oxymoron Roll-
regular or spicy- of a giant tempura shrimp with avocado, cucumber, lettuce,
tobiko & special sauce 8.95, Dragon's Eye Roll of maguro, asparagus, avocado
& tobiko 8.95, Philly Roll 8.95, Wasabi Balls 11.95, Green Dream Roll 10.95

Impressions:

A local surfer dude clued us in on this one. Up on the north end of Kapaa there's
a little storefront sushi restaurant called Wasabi's On The Reef. From the street
it doesn't look particularly special, but once you get inside, the place wins you
over. The menu has surprising range and depth, ultra fresh items line the sushi
case, and the wait staff couldn't be more congenial. As an added plus, the whole
experience can be had at both lunch and dinner.

Kauai Dining

West Side

Wrangler's Steakhouse
9852 Kaumualii Highway
Waimea, HI 96796
808-338-1218
Web: None
Hours: L 11:00 AM-4:00 PM Mo-Fr
        D 4:00 PM-9:00 PM Mo-Fr
        D 5:00 PM-9:00 PM Sa
Cards: AE MC V
Dress: Casual
Style: Sea/Stk $$$

Menu Sampler:

Breakfast:
N/A
Lunch:
Chicken Caesar Salad with grilled chicken slices, greens and garlic toast $8.95, Shrimp Louie with bay shrimp, egg, and fresh veggies $8.95, Wrangler Burger-grilled steak patty with mushrooms, cheese, onions and sprouts and steak fries $8.95, Kau Kau Tin with beef teriyaki, tempura shrimp and veggies $8.95, Pulehu Steak of grilled New York Steak with special garlic sauce $11.95
Dinner:
All entrees include soup & salad bar. Grilled Filet Mignon served on a sizzling platter $25, Rib Eye with peppercorn sauce $24, Grilled Sirloin Steak & Scampi $28, Pork Chops with crispy sweet & sour onions $18, Fresh Island Fish $Market Price, New York with zucchini, mushroom, onion & caper sauté $24, Steak & King Crab Legs $38, ahi with penne pasta, vegetables, bell pepper sauce $17, Shrimp Scampi with linguini pasta, garlic cream sauce $18
Desserts: Warm Peach Cobbler-vanilla bean ice cream $5.50, Flan $5.50

Impressions:

Wrangler's Steakhouse is located in the last town you pass through when driving to the Waimea Canyon. This restaurant is a wonderful addition to the west shore dining scene. It combines the area's picturesque past with an upscale menu. Better yet they do it at lunch as well as dinner. The focus might be steak and seafood, but it's done with flair and offers some local culinary treats as well. Look for high quality food and a cheerful wait staff. There's even a unique gift shop inside. This is a solid choice for visitors to this side of the island.

Kauai Dining

North Shore

Zelo's Beach House
Ching Young Village
5-8420 Kuhio Hwy (Hwy 56)
Hanalei, HI 96714
808-826-9700
www.zelosbeachhouse.com
Hours: LD 11:00 AM-9:30 PM
Cards: MC V
Dress: Casual
Style: Amer/Sea/Mex $$

Menu Sampler:

Breakfast:
N/A

Lunch/Dinner:
Pupus: Beer Battered Artichoke Hearts w/bleu cheese dip 9.95, Zelos Macho Nachos 10.95, Spicy Crab Cakes 11.95, Crispy Calamari 8.95, Tempura Dipped Sushi Roll 11.95, Thai Shrimp Leaf Wrap 10.95, Spinach & Artichoke Dip 9.95
Salads: Wild Organic Greens Salad $4.95, Classic Caesar 9.95, Mediterranean Salad 9.95, Asian Chicken Salad 12.95, Seafood Chowder 5.95/7.95
Sandwiches: Fresh Fish Burger 8.95, Zelo Burger 7.75, Fresh Ahi Tuna Salad Melt on rustic bun 9.50, NY Philly Cheese Steak Sandwich with bell pepper, onion & provolone 8.95, Chicken Parmesan Sandwich 8.95
Entrées: Seafood Risotto in a garlic basil broth over a bed of spinach & risotto 18.95, Pineapple Teriyaki Chicken served with grilled pineapple and jasmine rice 12.95, Zelos Famous Baby Back Ribs 18.95, New York Steak Roll Up-a choice strip thinly sliced then filled with mushrooms, gorgonzola cheese and roasted garlic, served with risotto cake and wilted spinach 18.95, Beer Battered Fish & Chips served with waffle fries 13.95, Local Fresh Fish $Mkt
Desserts: Mud Pie 5.95, Grasshopper Pie 5.95 Chocolate Suicide Cake 5.95

Impressions:

Zelo's might not be on a beach, but it's the kind of place people from the upper Midwest dream about when the Alberta Clipper starts blowing snow down their shorts. With its great tunes, large bar, casual atmosphere, and wide variety of tasty food, Zelo's fulfills many needs. This open-air establishment is a fun place to grab a quick lunch or spend an entire evening while visiting the north shore.

KAUAI DINING
BY REGION

KAUAI DINING BY REGION

West Side

South Shore

Lihue

East Coast

North Shore

FOOD & CULTURAL TERMS GLOSSARY

FOOD & CULTURAL TERMS GLOSSARY

a'a	rough clinker lava
aina	the land
abalone	large saltwater mollusk
aburage	deep-fried tofu
adobo	marinated Filipino chicken and/or pork stew
agemono	Japanese cooking method of preparing meats and vegetables by deep-frying
ahi	yellowfin tuna, often served raw as sashimi on a bed of Chinese cabbage with a wasabi and shoyu dipping sauce
ahupua'a	a land division used in old Hawaii consisting of all the lands between two adjoining ridges from the top of the mountain to the ocean
akamai	clever or smart
akua	spirit or god
ali'i	chief or noble
aloha	versatile term that can mean hello, good-bye, and love
Aloha Friday	casual dress day or more importantly the first day of the weekend party that actually starts Thursday afternoon
arroz	rice
arugula	peppery flavored greens
aumakua	guardian spirit
auntie	any older lady, a term of respect

'awa	kava, a beverage made from the ground roots of the intoxicating pepper
azuki	red beans
banh hoi	Vietnamese meat and vegetable roll-up
barbecue stick	char grilled teriyaki meat stick
bean curd	tofu
bean threads	fine thin noodles made from mung bean starch, long rice
bento	Japanese box lunch
black beans	fermented beans used in Chinese sauces
bok choy	a tall variety of cabbage with white celery like stems and dark green leaves
bulgoki	Korean teriyaki barbecue beef
bun	thin soft Vietnamese rice noodles
butterfish	black cod, has a smooth silky texture
carne	meat
cascaron	Filipino fried sweet dumpling
char siu	sweet marinated barbecued pork
chili oil	liquid fire made from chili peppers and oil
Chinese cabbage	a compact variety of cabbage with white celery-like stems and pale green leaves, also known as Napa cabbage or won bok
chorizo	hot and spicy sausage
chow	stir-fry
chow fun	cooked noodles combined with green onions and bits of meat or seafood then stir-fried with sesame oil

chun	Korean method of frying using flour followed by an egg wash
cilantro	Chinese parsley
coconut creme	thick creamy layer on top of a can of coconut milk
coconut milk	liquid extracted by squeezing grated coconut meat
crack seed	sweet or sour snack foods made from preserved fruits and seeds
da kine	what-cha-ma-call-it
daikon	large white Asian root vegetable commonly used as a garnish
dashi	broth made from dried seaweed and flakes of dried bonito
Diamond Head	directional term used on Oahu meaning to go east in the direction of Diamond Head or "Go Diamond Head"
dim sum	Chinese style dumplings
doce	sweet
donburi	thinly sliced meat, vegetables, and coddled egg served in a deep bowl over rice
edamame	lightly salted and boiled young soybeans
egg roll	fried pastry roll with various meat and vegetable fillings
Ewa	directional term used on Oahu meaning to go west in the direction of Ewa or "Go Ewa" which is opposite from Diamond Head and toward Pearl Harbor
fish cake	ground white fish, starch, and salt cooked together by steaming or frying
fish sauce	potent seasoning made from salt and fish

five spice powder	mixture of several spices that usually includes fennel, peppercorns, cinnamon, cloves, and star anise.
furikake	a dry condiment used on rice dishes
fusion cuisine	layers of flavor, texture, temperatures, and techniques created by combining elements from the cuisines of different cultures
ginger	spicy pungent root vegetable used as a flavoring in Asian cooking
gobo	burdock root
grinds	food
guava	sweet red tropical fruit
guisates	Filipino pork or chicken dish made with peas and pimento in a tomato based sauce
hale	house or building
halo halo	tropical fruit sundae made with ice, milk and sugar instead of ice cream
ham har	fermented dried shrimp paste, very funky, a little goes a long way
hana	work
hana hou	do it one more time/encore!
haole	Caucasian
hapa	half as in hapa-haole or half-Caucasian
haupia	coconut custard dessert
Hawaii Regional Cuisine	movement started in the late '80's/early '90's by young local chefs combining island cooking styles and classic techniques with fresh local products to create an exciting new fusion cuisine

Hawaiian chili water	liquid heat made with Hawaiian chili peppers, water, and salt
Hawaiian rock salt	coarse white or pink rock salt
Hawaiian time	later rather than sooner
heiau	ancient Hawaiian stone temple
hekka	a stir-fry dish made with meat and vegetables in a shoyu-based sauce
hibachi	small charcoal cooker
hoisin sauce	thick, sweet, but pungent sauce used in Chinese cooking
holoholo	pleasure trip, to go "holoholo"
hono	bay
honu	turtle
hukilau	pulling of a large fish net by a group
hui	club or association
hula	Hawaiian native dance
huli huli	"turn turn" as in grilling chicken
imu	Hawaiian underground oven made by digging a pit and lining it with hot lava rocks covered by banana plants and food and burying it for several hours, used at luaus for making kalua pork, laulau, sweet potatoes, etc.
inari sushi	cone sushi made by filling fried tofu pockets with sweet vinegar flavored rice
ipo	sweetheart
kaffir lime leaves	leaves of the kaffir lime tree used as flavoring in Thai cooking

kahuna	priest or skilled person
kai	the sea
kaiseki	Japanese fine dining in courses
kal bi ribs	Korean teriyaki beef short ribs
kale	Portuguese cabbage
kalo	taro
kalua pork	shredded pork prepared luau style in an imu pit, also known locally as kalua pig
kama'aina	long time resident or someone who was born in Hawaii
kamaboko	Japanese fish cake
kane	man
kapu	forbidden
kapuna	grandparent or wise older person
katsu	breaded cutlet
kau kau	food, a place to eat
keiki	child
kiawe	dry land hardwood used in smoking and grilling meats
ki'i	statue or image
kim chee	spicy Korean condiment made from fermented cabbage and peppers
koa	valuable hardwood tree, warrior
Koko Head	directional term used on Oahu meaning to go in the direction of Koko Head or "Go Koko Head"
kokua	help

kona	leeward
kona wind	muggy airflow from the equator
kukui	candlenut tree, the source of kukui nut oil
Kula	a truck gardening district in Upcountry Maui
kulolo	sweet pudding made with poi
kumu	teacher as in kumu hula
lanai	deck or patio
lau hala	woven mats
lau lau	flavored meat mixed with taro leaves and wrapped in ti leaves then steamed, often in an imu
laver	purple seaweed used in making nori
lechon	roasted pig
lei	garland of flowers
lemon grass	woody lemon flavored grass used as flavoring in Southeast Asian cooking
li hing mui	sweet and sour seasoning made from dried plums and salt
lilikoi	passion fruit
limu	edible seaweed
linguica	spicy Portuguese pork sausage seasoned with garlic and paprika
loa	long
loco moco	local dish consisting of rice, a large hamburger patty or slices of Spam, and fried eggs with lots of brown gravy over all
lolo	crazy

107

lomi	to knead or massage
lomi lomi salmon	salted salmon finely diced with tomatoes and green onions
long rice	clear noodles cooked in broth
lua	restroom
luau	Hawaiian feast, also a dish made from taro leaves, coconut crème, and meat
lulu	calm
lumpia	fried spring roll with meat, vegetable, or dessert fillings
lup cheong	Chinese pork sausage
lychee	sweet white fruit
macadamia nuts	small round nut with creamy but crunchy texture
mac salad	macaroni and mayonnaise
mahalo	thank you
mainland	North America
makai	directional term that is helpful on an island meaning to turn or look toward the ocean
maki sushi	sushi rolled in nori
malasada	wonderful sweet brought here by the Portuguese similar to a fresh sugar donut but minus the hole
malihini	newcomer
malo	loincloth
mana	power or energy from the spirit world
manapua	steamed pork bun

mandoo	Korean dumplings with meat and vegetable fillings
mango	golden fleshed tropical fruit
mano	shark
Manoa	a gardening district near Honolulu, the Manoa Valley
mauka	directional term meaning to look or turn toward the mountain or uphill part of an island
mauna	mountain
mein	Chinese noodles
mele	chant or song
menehune	legendary "little people" of Hawaii
mirin	sweet rice cooking wine
miso	fermented soybean paste
miso soup	light Japanese soup made from soybean paste and garnished with tofu, kamaboko, daikon, green onions, and wakame
mixed plate	plate lunch version of a mixed grill
moa	native Polynesian chicken
moana	ocean
mochi	rice cake
mochiko	sweet rice flour
mo'o	lizard or water spirit
musubi	rice ball
muu muu	loose fitting ankle length dress

naan	Indian flatbread
nabemono	Japanese cooking method of preparing thin slices of meat and vegetables in a hot broth
'Nalo	As in Waimanalo, a garden district on the Windward side of Oahu
nam pla	Thai fish sauce
nam prik	Thai hot sauce
nani	beautiful
nene	Hawaiian goose
nigiri sushi	oblong sushi
niu	coconut
noni	native shrub bearing medicinal fruit
nori	roasted seaweed pressed into sheets
norimaki	sushi rolled in nori
nui	big or great
nuoc mam	Vietnamese fish sauce
off-island	in the islands one does not go "out of town" they go "off-island"
ogo	type of seaweed favored by the Japanese
ohana	extended family
ohelo	native shrub bearing edible berries
okazuya	a Japanese delicatessen where fast foods and snacks are served buffet style
ono	delicious
opae	shrimp

opihi	Hawaiian escargot harvested from rocks along the ocean and eaten raw with salt
oyster sauce	thick brown sauce made from oysters and shoyu often used in stir fry dishes
Pacific Rim Cuisine	a fusion of cuisines involving methods and ingredients from the countries around the Pacific Ocean
pad thai	Thai noodles
pahoehoe	smooth ropey lava
pakalolo	crazy smoke, marijuana, buds; something to decline when offered
pali	cliff
pancit	Filipino noodles
paniolo	Hawaiian cowboy
panko	Japanese breadcrumbs
pao	bread
pao doce	Portuguese sweet bread
papaya	smooth skinned orange-fleshed tropical fruit that can also be used green when peeled and shredded in a salad
pasteles	similar to a tamale except made with bananas instead of corn flour
patis	Filipino fish sauce
pau	finished
pau hana	finished working
pho	Vietnamese noodle soup
pidgin	Hawaiian Creole English
pipi kaula	Hawaiian beef jerky

plantain	cooking banana
plate lunch	island style blue plate special with a main entrée such as teriyaki beef or chicken, two scoops of white rice, and a scoop of macaroni salad
poi	glutinous paste made by pounding steamed taro root, the Hawaiian staple starch
poke	ceviche dish made with cubed fish or sliced octopus mixed with onion and seaweed then marinated in shoyu and spices
pono	righteous
ponzu	tart Japanese citrus sauce
Portuguese sausage	spicy garlic and paprika flavored pork sausage, linguica
pua	flower
pua'a	pig
pueo	owl
puka	hole
pupu	appetizer
pu'u	hill
ramen	curly Japanese wheat noodles
rice noodle	noodles made with rice flour
rice paper	round rice flour wrapper that is soaked in hot water to soften before use
saimin	island noodle soup that has many variations and broths--extras may include Spam, teriyaki beef, green onions, vegetables, hard-cooked eggs, and fish cake

sake	Japanese rice wine
sashimi	raw fish sliced very thin and served with spicy condiments and dipping sauce
satay	tender chicken or beef strips marinated in coconut milk and spices then skewered and grilled
sesame oil	aromatic oil made from sesame seeds used sparingly to flavor Asian dishes
shabu shabu	chafing dish cookery involving thinly sliced meats and vegetables simmered in broth usually with a tabletop preparation
shaka	hand signal using the thumb and little finger used as a greeting
shave ice	similar to a snow cone except there is no crunch as the ice is shaved instead of crushed, can be topped with wonderful tropical flavored syrups and served with ice cream and azuki beans
shoyu	Japanese soy sauce, Aloha Brand is preferred in the islands as it is not as salty as some other types
soba	Japanese buckwheat noodles
somen	thin Japanese wheat noodles
Spam	canned spiced pork lunchmeat
spring roll	fried rice paper roll with various fillings
starch	rice or potatoes
sukiyaki	Japanese beef, tofu, vegetable, and noodle dish with shoyu based sauce commonly cooked at the table
summer roll	fresh rice paper roll with various fillings
sushi	small slices of vegetables, fruits, fish, or meat combined with tangy rice

sweet bread	rich egg bread commonly called Molokai or Portuguese sweet bread
sweet rice	also known as sticky rice or glutinous rice
tako	octopus
talk story	to have a casual conversation
tapa	cloth made from pounded tree bark
taro	starchy root plant used in making poi
teri	teriyaki
teishoku	a complete Japanese meal including soup, salad, entrée, pickled vegetables, and rice
tempura	meat, seafood, or vegetables fried in a light batter coating
tendon	meat and vegetable tempura served over rice
teppanyaki	Japanese cooking method of grilling vegetables, seafood, meat and rice tableside by a knife-wielding chef, very entertaining
teriyaki	sweet tangy shoyu based marinade
Thai basil	herb used in Thai cooking, has a purple flower and sharper taste than sweet basil
ti	broad-leafed plant whose leaves are used for plates, hula skirts, and for wrapping foods and religious offerings
tobiko	flying fish roe, caviar
tofu	soybean curd available fresh or fermented
tom yum	spicy Thai soup
tonkatsu	fried cutlet
tsukemono	pickled vegetables

tuong ot	Vietnamese hot sauce
tutu	grandmother
two scoop rice	two scoops of cooked white rice
uala	sweet potato
udon	thick Japanese wheat noodles
ulu	breadfruit
vertical food	a physical manifestation of fusion cuisine where the elements of the dish are stacked
wahine	woman
wai	water
wakame	a seaweed condiment
wasabi	spicy Japanese horseradish paste often combined sparingly with shoyu to make a dipping sauce for sushi and sashimi
wiki wiki	hurry up, very fast
wok	round bottomed cooking pot used over very high heat to quick sear or stir-fry chopped meats and vegetables
won bok	Chinese cabbage
won ton	Chinese meat dumplings
wor	vegetables
yakimono	Japanese cooking method of preparing meats and vegetables by broiling or grilling
yakiniku	tabletop grilling
yakisoba	grilled noodles
yakitori	grilled meat and vegetable kebabs

HAWAIIAN FISH & SEAFOOD GLOSSARY

HAWAIIAN FISH & SEAFOOD GLOSSARY

Hawaii IS the island state and what could be a more fitting headliner on a Hawaiian menu than the bounty of the sea? Just like everything else found in this Pacific paradise there are unique spins to the fish and seafood offerings. With this in mind we have created a separate glossary to help you explore and better appreciate the aquatic offerings found in Hawaii's dining spots.

Visitors need to be aware that finfish are nearly always listed by their Hawaiian names on island menus. That's no problem for those who grew up in Hawaii, but the rest of us would do well to brush up on the subject first. How else would you know that an ahi is a prize big eye or yellow fin tuna, and that a tako isn't the same as a taco? The word tako in Hawaii means octopus, and receiving one instead of the other could come as quite a surprise!

Most people don't realize that longliners stay out for several days at a time, but trollers come in every night and that the difference in the quality and freshness of their catch can be noticed. If you are paying for fresh island fish you want to make sure that you get it. You might see the term "day boat" used in some of the finer restaurants to describe the freshest of fresh fish and seafood. Regardless, make sure to ask and always insist on fish that has never been frozen.

As long as we're on the subject of getting what you're paying for, let's take a look at the economics of fish and seafood in Hawaii. There's a misconception that just because people see "water water everywhere", the aquatic resources must be limitless and the prices low. Nothing could be farther from the truth. The high cost of production through aquaculture and harvest in the wild along with huge local and foreign demand drive prices to the upper limit of the menu.

In closing, when you decide to take the plunge and go out for fish or seafood, make it a point to trust the recommendations at the restaurant. The chef knows how to match species and preparations for the best possible results. Just let your waiter know what you have in mind and listen to his suggestions. You'll be far happier in the end if you go with the flow than if you try to have it your way.

ahi	big eye or yellow fin tuna
aku	skipjack tuna, most common spring through early fall, robust flavor, firm texture, often served as poke or in sushi, primarily caught by commercial pole-and-line fishermen and recreational trollers
akule	big-eyed scad, a local favorite, primarily caught by netting or by hook-and-line fishermen

119

ama ebi	sweet shrimp or langoustines, harvested with traps from deep water, available locally but often imported
a'u	billfish of any type
big eye ahi	big eye tuna, most common from mid-fall through mid-spring, moderate beef-like flavor, medium firm texture, favored for sashimi and poke, primarily caught by long-line boats
ehu	red snapper, moderate flavor, most common during winter, medium firm texture, primarily caught by deepwater hook-and-line fishermen
hapu'upu'u	grouper or sea bass, most common spring and fall, moderate flavor, medium firm texture, primarily caught by deepwater hook-and-line fishermen
hebi	shortbill spearfish, most common mid-spring through early fall, moderate flavor, medium firm texture, primarily caught by commercial long-line boats
kajiki	pacific blue marlin, most common summer through fall, moderate flavor, firm texture, primarily caught by commercial long-line boats and recreational trollers
Keahole lobster	clawed "Maine" lobsters raised on the Big Island through aquaculture, available all year
Kona lobster	spiny or rock lobster, primarily caught by divers working the reef or by trapping, usually imported, available all year
lehi	silver mouth snapper, most common during late fall and winter, moderate flavor, medium texture, primarily caught by deepwater hook-and-line fishermen

mahimahi	dolphinfish, most common spring and fall, moderate almost sweet flavor, medium texture, ask if the fish is fresh "island fish", primarily caught by commercial and recreational trollers
moi	pacific threadfin, the royal fish, now raised locally through aquaculture, mild flavor, delicate texture, available all year
monchong	bigscale or sickle pomfret, available all year, robust flavor, medium firm texture, primarily caught as a by-catch of tuna long-liners and deepwater hook-and-line fishermen.
nairagi	striped marlin, most common winter and spring, moderate flavor, medium firm texture, primarily caught by commercial long-line boats and recreational trollers
onaga	ruby or long-tailed red snapper, most common late fall and winter, mild flavor, medium texture, primarily caught by deepwater hook-and-line fishermen
ono	wahoo, most common late spring through early fall, mild almost citrus-like flavor, medium firm texture, primarily caught by commercial and recreational trollers with part of the catch harvested by commercial long-line fishermen
opae	shrimp, now raised locally through aquaculture, available all year
opah	moonfish, most common spring through summer, robust flavor, medium texture, primarily caught by commercial long-line fishermen fishing over seamounts
opakapaka	crimson snapper, most common fall and winter, mild flavor, delicate texture, primarily caught by deepwater hook-and-line fishermen

opihi

small limpet, found on coastal rock faces in the surf zone, eaten raw with salt as "Hawaiian escargot"

papio

juvenile pompano or crevally, medium flavor, firm texture, caught by shore casters, shallow water trollers, and bottom fishermen

shutome

broadbill swordfish, most common spring and summer, moderate flavor, medium firm texture, caught at night by commercial long-line fishermen

tako

octopus or squid, primarily caught by divers working in shallow water or by jigging

tombo

albacore or "white meat" tuna, most common mid-spring through mid-fall, moderate flavor, medium texture, primarily caught by commercial long-line fishermen and small-boat hand line fishermen

uku

grey snapper, most common mid-spring through mid-fall, moderate flavor, medium firm texture, primarily caught in deep water by hook-and-line fishermen but is also caught near the surface by recreational trollers

ula

spiny or rock lobster, primarily caught by divers working the reef or by trapping

ula papapa

slipper lobster, primarily caught by divers working the reef or by trapping

ulua

adult pompano or crevally, medium flavor, firm texture, caught by shore casters, shallow water trollers, and bottom fishermen

yellow fin ahi

yellow fin tuna, most common mid-spring through mid-fall, moderate beef-like flavor, medium firm texture, favored for sashimi and poke, primarily caught by commercial long-line boats and commercial and recreational trollers